DA

What a Way to Make a Living!
Tales of a Small-Town Veterinarian

DR. STEVE PEARSON

DEDICATION

To all of my grandchildren. I hope this helps you to know
who your Granddaddy was before you knew him.

At the time of this writing, we have thirteen grandchildren:
Allie, Luke, Nathan, Seth, Margaret, Birti, Megan,
Penelope, Rosemary, Sam, Bethany, Silas, and Enoch.

CONTENTS

DR. STEVE PEARSON

PREFACE

"Why add another book to the stack of existing ones about life as a veterinarian?" That's a question I needed to answer before writing the first words of this book.

Allow me to answer it with the top motivators for me:

- I wanted to leave a record for my grandchildren to read that would help them understand who their Granddaddy was before they knew me.

- I hope many former clients will smile as they remember bringing pets into our hospital and interacting with our staff.

- Maybe some young person who's considering the pursuit of a DVM degree will learn some insights they hadn't previously thought about, and this realistic account will help them make the right decision.

- Above all, I hope that as you read, you'll be able

to feel the *joie de vivre* that characterized the days at our little veterinary practice in Hartselle, Alabama. Every person I've spent time with in reminiscing about those days reacts with a smile, a giggle, or outright laughter as memories flood back.

Finding the right words will be difficult. Is it possible to construct the sentences, the paragraphs, and the chapters in ways that allow readers to sense the depth of rich relationships developing through events that occurred over a period of three decades?

I hope it is possible because we lived in the midst of extraordinary days. Even the challenges, the failures, and the losses became building blocks. We worked together within a unique identity that we all understood. We trusted each other and defended each other when necessary.

The regulatory environment surrounding the practice of veterinary medicine was very different then. For example, we were able to start a business from scratch in ways that would not be acceptable nowadays.

The lack of emergency and referral hospitals mandated the local veterinarian to perform surgeries and procedures that we refer to a specialist in these modern times. That environment allowed for some stretching of my capabilities. Finding those limits and realizing I could accomplish more than I thought I could gave me fertile ground for a gratifying life.

My days at Pearson Animal Hospital (PAH) came in an era when veterinarians enjoyed a high level of public trust and esteem. Word-of-mouth was the primary engine for growth. People held a high degree of appreciation for honesty, integrity, and amiability. They depended on veterinarians for medical information back then because there was no internet at their fingertips.

I cannot imagine any way I'd rather have spent my most productive years than practicing veterinary medicine at Pearson Animal Hospital in Hartselle, Alabama. Even though we were not born or raised in Hartselle, Connie and I firmly consider it our home. It is home to Laura, Matt, and Julie in the most real sense. We love Hartselle and the people who live here.

We also dearly love the people God sent our way to work alongside me. Vicky Sharrott, Kathy Jenkins, Jennifer Garner, Brenda Hall, Becca King, and Carrie Wallace combined to work well over fifty years at PAH. The fun, the hard work, and the heartwarming relationships we enjoyed could fill a much more extensive book.

Dr. Phil Gault came along as a partner during the last ten years of my PAH time. We are alike in many ways and entirely different in some ways. Those traits fit together to form an excellent professional team. What I fondly remember most is our almost daily discussions at the end of work days, sitting back in the study solving the world's problems. Though serious at times, we laughed ourselves to tears more days than I can count. Those times enriched my life.

Dr. David Crouch grew up before my eyes while his family and ours attended church together. God had a long-range plan. The day Connie and I signed the papers transferring PAH to Dr. Gault and Dr. Crouch represented evidence of His caring for each of us in ways we couldn't see before.

1 THE SEEDS OF A CALLING

"For I know the plans I have for you," declares the Lord, "plans for welfare and not for evil, to give you a future and a hope." Jeremiah 29:11

There is no way to describe what I was feeling for the first time in my life. It was a dark feeling. It was a helpless and hopeless feeling. Yes, the heavy pressing of guilt was there, too. For a few seconds or moments – I can't say how long – I felt paralyzed and what to do next would not come to me.

I had just witnessed from a distance of only a few steps the cruel and painful death of my friend and buddy, Barney. Only a few minutes before, he'd been bouncing around my feet, wildly wagging his tail, panting with a playful smile. As the car sped away, Barney's body lay lifeless, nothing left but a warm, mangled clump of fur crumpled up on cold asphalt.

Barney was not my first pet. Memories of other pets

flooded my mind, compounding the pain of losing him that day. There were two special dogs named Blackie and Moog in my life before Barney. Those two left before their time, too, but in different ways. Letting go of Blackie and Moog had its challenges for sure, but the end for them came with some warning.

Although Blackie was not my first pet dog, he came along at an age where my memories are much more reliable than those of others before him. He was a black and white Cocker Spaniel with long, curly hair and, of course, those typical smelly ears.

I grew up in a middle-class neighborhood in Decatur, Alabama, at a time when all the kids played outdoors every day, no matter the weather. As a puppy, Blackie gained some notoriety by getting his picture in the local newspaper. The front page picture included Blackie, my little brother, our pet rabbit, and me as we fed them both in the same bowl. Just a few short days later, we discovered furry rabbit parts scattered all over the backyard – the only evidence of Blackie's latest meal.

Our house sat on a small lot bordered on each side by neighbors, a street in the front, and a gravel alley on the back side. Blackie's dog house sat along the edge of a fenced area near the alley. There were huge sweet gum trees all around giving him plenty of shade during hot summer days. We bonded deeply with Blackie as he traced our steps and kept us company while we built tiny roads in the dirt with toy bulldozers and trucks.

Over time, a terrible problem developed for Blackie and our family. It was no fault of his. Our neighborhood had a preponderance of young, restless boys who were always searching for entertainment. A penned up Cocker Spaniel near the alley turned out to be an irresistible target of taunting with sticks and small rocks when boys "from down the street" passed by his pen. As the days and weeks passed by, Blackie's response became more and more vicious. Changes in his personality led to grave concern in my parents' minds about who he might bite if the opportunity ever arose. Mom and Dad's explanation for Blackie's sudden disappearance almost convinced us that he had found a new home with a loving family "way out in the country" somewhere. We were sure that he was now a much happier dog. I never heard more about him, and I never pressed them for more information.

Moog was a black and white, medium-sized mixed breed dog who just showed up at our house one day and decided to hang around. Moog got his name from a book I was reading at the time, so my attachment to him melded quickly and deeply. He was around long enough to learn a few tricks and, it seemed to me, to develop a growing degree of loyalty. It was a sad day when Moog's rightful owner spotted him and me playing in our front yard. Of course, when I saw the delight in both Moog and his owner, the only option was to try and be happy about their reunion. It took me a long time to reconcile it all emotionally.

I'm sure lots of people have similar experiences to tell about the highs and lows of bonding with a pet. So it's not the stories themselves that prompted me to write about them. Their significance lies in the parts they played in my finding my way to my calling in life. I had not even the remotest idea at the time my calling would be to veterinary medicine. The truth is, at the time I couldn't tell you the difference between a veterinarian and an animal control officer! I guess I thought that because I'd seen what we called "dog catchers" back then, but not a vet.

Nothing happens in life without a reason. The happy

and sad times as a child bonding with pets became a foundation for my career – a lifelong calling I did not know was coming my way. Unknown to me, there would be countless times when a client with a sick or injured pet would need empathy from their pet's doctor more than anything else. Experiences during my early years with pets, I believe, happened because of the One who knew His plan for me. Though I didn't know it, I was learning first-hand the intensity of the bond between humans and animals.

Still, the road to my calling was not straight or smooth. Nearing the end of the second year of courses at Auburn University, I applied for entrance into the School of Veterinary Medicine. There were scores of applicants for each seat in the 1968 freshman class. Many of those applicants carried one or two degrees into the interview process. Many of them had the advantage of birth into families with close relatives who were practicing veterinarians. Most had worked or volunteered in hometown veterinary clinics. None of those characteristics were true of me. I just believed this was the path I'd been led to follow.

When I received a letter of acceptance into vet school, there was yet another huge hurdle left to clear safely. Its name was Organic Chemistry II. Without a good grade on the final exam, my grade point average could fall below the standard required to enter vet school. The exam fell on a Thursday morning, so I alerted my church family back home to pray for me as I prepared for the test. As foolish as it seems now, I'd made up my mind to pursue something else if this didn't work out.

I somehow did well on an exam that truly seemed like Goliath to me. That crisis became a personal spiritual marker for years to come, a marker I could remember on trying days and remind myself that I was doing what God wanted me to be doing.

As soon as I cleared that hurdle, a dark secret gripped me with fear. It's a secret almost no one has ever known about me until now. But, I must tell it now so all will see, as I have, how faithful God is to His promise to "never leave or forsake you."

Pretty much every time I'd get a vaccination, an injection, or have blood drawn, I passed out cold. And there was no way I could even watch someone else get those, either, without hitting the floor. How in the world would I ever function as a doctor? I'd never been tested to see what my reaction might be when an animal was involved. Still, I pressed on with faith that I was indeed on the right path.

The freshman year of vet school meant spending hours of gouging through cadavers in anatomy class. No problem. Course after course involved in-depth study of blood and guts. I continued to be fine, but the fear remained. Eventually, surgery classes appeared on my schedule. I made it, and realized I could do this! Did the fear disappear? No, it didn't, but I was gaining some confidence.

Another crisis came when Dr. Robert Horne asked me to assist him in the surgical excision of a massive tumor on the chest of an old Chihuahua. As head of the surgery department, Dr. Horne was nationally known and respected in veterinary circles. What if HE found out about my secret? As it turned out, I had to admit to a puzzling degree of enjoyment during that procedure. I had yet another spiritual marker.

Fighting fear with faith became a consistent routine

over the next several years. Hardly a day passed without a skirmish between fear and faith. Now I can look back over more than 36 years of practicing veterinary medicine while overcoming a very real battle day after day.

I want you to know this so it can serve as evidence of the grace, mercy, and care God gives to His children. Where He leads, He provides.

I needed a confidence booster, a cheerleader, a motivator, and unconditional love. God provided all that and infinitely more all wrapped up in one person. You'll meet her in the next chapter.

2 WHY HARTSELLE?

Delight yourself also in the Lord, and He shall give you the desires of your heart. Psalm 37:4

"I think I'd like to open a practice in either Hartselle, Alabama, or somewhere in Australia."

Yes, I was serious when those words came out of my mouth. But that was way out of character for me. I've always required a lot of prodding to get out of my comfort zone. No doubt, those words were from a lovesick boy trying to impress his soon-to-be wife. Together we made the decision and decided to see how things went in Hartselle first.

Connie and I got married just days before the beginning of my senior year in vet school. She'd been at Samford University for three years. Our wedding took place on March 20, 1971, in a small church in Decatur crowded with family and friends. She transferred to Auburn without losing any credits and finished her degree in piano performance in December 1971.

She knew nothing about veterinary medicine, and I knew less than that about music. That was about to change for both of us, of course. It meant I'd get my first exposure to classical music, and she'd get her first experiences of eating dinner with a man who reeked of barnyard odors.

Our marriage came at just the right stage of my veterinary education. The bookwork was behind me, and practical, hands-on veterinary medicine waited straight ahead. Gradually, I began to understand that I was responsible for the well-being of the one I loved and cherished. Connie believed in me far more than anyone else ever did. That combination of responsibility and genuine encouragement from Connie enabled me to acclimate to life as a veterinarian.

The final year of vet school passed quickly, and we found that married life was even better than we'd imagined it would be. The fact that our callings were so different added to the richness of our relationship. The end of each day found us energetically sharing our contrasting encounters and events of the day.

In a flash, we were standing on the tiny front porch of a duplex apartment in the old Five Points district of Huntsville, Alabama. We'd gone there because I was doing my preceptorship. (It's comparable to an internship for medical doctors.) We were there so I could work with a seasoned and respected veterinary practice owner named Dr. Robert Bentley. Although the official term was for three months, we ended up staying for a full year.

Once again, God had led me to the perfect place. Dr. Bentley was a kind, soft-spoken man who taught me more about animals from tiny kittens to 2-ton bulls than the summation of what I'd learned in four years at Auburn.

More importantly, he demonstrated integrity and compassion toward clients of all kinds. I knew that the more I could imitate him, the more successful I would be in the long-run.

By the end of that year, Connie and I were ready to step out on our own and develop a life that was uniquely ours. The time was right for opening a practice in Hartselle. There was only one other vet in town, and he was not far from retirement. Farm animal doctors were scarce, and local pet owners had grown tired of driving to Decatur for veterinary services.

Be careful who your mentors are.

Years later, when I was independently practicing in Hartselle, I'd found myself using mannerisms picked up from Dr. Bentley. For example, after finishing his examination and prescribing medications to a client, he'd lean back against the counter, smile, hold his chin with one hand, and ask, "Now Mrs. So-and-So, do you think you'll be able to apply that cream to Daisy's ear canal twice a day?" It was his way to assure clients that he was in no hurry to get to the next patient and that the client could relax and talk with him like a family member or close friend. That's one of the ways he taught me to enjoy life as a veterinarian.

Not only that, but when we built a hospital in Hartselle, the layout mimicked that of Bentley Animal Hospital. Nothing fancy, but oh so efficient! Forty-two years later, Pearson Animal Hospital is still functional and practical.

PAH started out very tiny.

The day was bright and sunny, but still chilly and windy, like mid-March days in North Alabama tend to be. Connie and I were on our fourth stop at garage sales when she spotted a plain wooden desk and accompanying spindle back chair. With a little dusting off, the pale green paint finish gave it a relaxed and inviting quality. All four legs were sturdy, and it was small enough to fit well into what was to become our reception and waiting room.

I can assure you, at this point in our journey, we did our shopping by looking at the price before considering any purchase. Somehow, we ended the day with the desk, a chair, a functional patent-leather 3-seat sofa, and a money box.

That small, gray, metal moneybox (as we called it) turned out to be incredibly durable. It was a far cry from the bulky cash register I'd seen my grandparents use in their clothing store, but we were sure it was sufficient for the short term. At least a dozen years of busy practice must have passed before we gave in and replaced it with a larger one with a compartmental tray for separating cash, coins, and checks. I want to kick myself for letting it get away and not keeping it as a reminder of our roots.

On April 2, 1973, we opened for business on Main Street in Hartselle. I'd used a stencil to paint PEARSON ANIMAL HOSPITAL in white letters on the dark red four-foot long plywood sign. It hung over the door to our 3-room rented office space. It was one of four units in a small office complex. Other businesses there included a real estate office and an insurance agency.

A few steps from Main Street, the front door opened into the reception room. The middle room served as the examination, treatment, surgery, and radiology departments. It had cabinets on one wall hanging conveniently over counter space where we placed the microscope from my days in vet school. There was a used refrigerator standing beside another wall. Other than the ancient, WWII vintage portable x-ray machine donated by Dr. Bentley, our equipment was new. I'd purchased brand new metal surgical instruments, an examination/surgery table, a gas anesthesia machine, and a blood analyzer just like the ones we used at Bentley Animal Hospital.

Opening the door to room number three revealed a bank of five shiny metal cages for boarding, grooming, and hospitalized patients. That room was finished out with an old, claw-foot bathtub we used for bathing and dipping patients.

I parked a 1962 red and white Chevy pickup truck out back on the gravel alley between the building and Nasty Branch, which ran through downtown Hartselle. Attached snugly behind the two-door cab was a white toolbox filled with equipment for farm animal work.

Thanks to a new friend I'd met at church, I'd already made calls to several local farms in that truck in the weeks leading up to our official opening. Earl Cook was a well-known cattle farmer who gave me a big boost by introducing me to other farmers who needed veterinary services. He'll come up again later in the story.

Connie, my musician wife, became our first receptionist and vet assistant. She may not have known a lot about veterinary medicine, but she sure knew how to treat people well and build lasting relationships. Even though her tenure at Pearson Animal Hospital was short, her demeanor helped us develop a nucleus of loyal clients. Many of them are still friends today.

Two landmark events occurred on our first official day of business. The significance of one was apparent immediately. The importance of the other would unfold over three decades.

I was pacing the floor as I waited for Connie to return from her doctor appointment. For farm calls, I always kept my brown coveralls zipped up so that only the knot of my necktie was visible. Black rubber boots made their distinct sounds with each anxious step. A farm client called while she was gone, and I didn't want to keep him waiting. It seemed risky to close the office and leave the phone unattended, and I knew she should return at any moment. Why did she have to see a doctor on our very first day of business, anyway? Balancing work and life is never easy for a practicing veterinarian.

When she finally came through the door, I knew the farm call would have to wait a little longer. Something was different. Her face showed a combination of concern and joy that I'd never seen before. Why she had to tell me, I'll never know. The reason for her expression should have been so obvious. I was about to begin learning how to make my family a priority over my profession. At least I did stop pacing long enough to hear her say, "We're having a baby!"

Immediately, hugging and dancing and laughing erupted in that little room right on Main Street. If we could have known anything about the little one who'd arrive on November 1, 1973, our hearts could not have contained the joy.

I didn't say it to her, but after a little reality set in, I was thinking to myself, "What? You're telling me this on our very first day? We don't even know how we're gonna pay the bills and eat this month!"

My motivation to succeed doubled in an instant. From that moment to this, our family has been the reason behind working hard and serving clients with integrity. Nothing else could have been a stronger motivation, and nothing else could have promised comparable rewards.

Later that day, the other landmark, our first small animal client, walked into the front door. Mrs. Andre Reed was holding a black mixed-breed dog named Inky. A soft-spoken, widowed nurse, Mrs. Reed was the embodiment of the perfect client. She was pleasant, kept a permanent smile, and demonstrated trust in my abilities from the very beginning. Because of her ability to care for animals, most of her visits were for minor health issues and preventive care like vaccinations and parasite control. I didn't know it then, but she also loved cats and always showed up on time for all their appointments. If only I could have cloned her that day into a few hundred more just like her, we'd have been set for life!

By the way, the reason she was such a landmark is that almost thirty years later, she and a couple of cats would come in for my last appointment at PAH.

Morning sickness during that first pregnancy didn't mix well with odors associated with animals, scented air fresheners, and smoking clients. Connie was soon to give up her business functions to some new faces. We were on the verge of the best years anyone could hope to live through.

There'll be more stories from the two-plus years PAH operated from those three rooms. But we soon outgrew their capacity and built an actual veterinary hospital on Highway 31 near the high school.

Our family soon grew, too. By October 1978, the two of us had become the five of us.

3 PEOPLE WHO GOT US STARTED

For by wise guidance you can wage your war, and
in abundance of counselors, there is victory.
Proverbs 24:6

Now to Him who is able to do far more abundantly
than all that we ask or think, according to the
power at work within us, …. Ephesians 4:20

The ease and speed at which a new business can be
born in today's Internet world seem incredible. Come up
with a product (real or virtual), connect with millions of
people through multiple social media outlets, send a few
emails and *voila*, you're in business.

That's great. I hope it never stops. But the downside
is the absence of close, lasting relationships with clients
and customers. I doubt there is a profession which lends
itself to those kinds of relationships better than practicing
veterinary medicine in a small town. I hope that never

changes, either.

Obviously, in 1973 the Internet was waiting in the distant future, and most businesses relied on word-of-mouth for sustained growth. Besides, blatant advertising was still considered unethical for medical professions.

When we moved to Hartselle, I did not know a soul who lived there, but there was a need for a veterinary practice in the area. Such opportunities are much more difficult to find nowadays. We were fortunate to be in the right place at a good time.

Still, being the introvert that I am, help was needed if many folks were going to become aware of our presence. God provided an all-star team of advocates.

The following is only a partial list. There were many, many others, too. These are the ones who made deep impressions that are still fresh in my mind all these years later.

Earl Cook

Earl was an outgoing, funny, larger than life man who spread the word and encouraged me when I needed it most.

Earl supported his wife and two sons by spreading lime and fertilizer for area farmers and by managing a large herd of cattle. Those sons of his sure came in handy for herding cows, calves, and bulls through the chute while I gave vaccines, de-wormers, and performed pregnancy checks.

Earl claimed he could tell a lot about a cow's reproductive cycle by observing what he termed "her pocketbook." Not exactly a professional term, but his theory was right-on.

I'll never know how Earl heard I was coming to town, but long before opening the office, he distributed my phone number to several cattle and dairy farmers. Of course, that resulted in some valuable work and income sooner than I'd expected.

I was never shy about collecting my fee on the spot because our young business didn't have the cash flow to allow working on credit. One day after Earl handed me a check for treating a couple of cases of pinkeye, he asked me, "Want to know what folks are saying about you?" I nervously choked out a "Yeah, sure" not knowing what I might be about to learn. He said, "They all like the work you do for them, but they're surprised you don't charge more for it." That was a tremendous encouragement! The main thing I heard was, "They like your work." Plus, if they perceived they were getting more than their money's worth, I was right where I wanted to be.

John Tomlinson

John was a young accountant who worked for a local CPA. He was assigned to take care of the new vet and his tiny new business. I'm thankful he was because when he opened his independent office, we followed him and began a long-term friendship.

John managed a small cattle herd, too. I'll never forget his favorite comment about the cattle business. He'd say with a wry smile, "I know there's money in cattle farming…because I've put a lot of money into it."

He was a typical example of most of my clients who were investing in cattle at the time. The price of beef cattle experienced a sharp rise just about the time our practice opened, so most everyone who had an acre or two of land decided to get in on the boon. Many of those investors already had "day jobs" and raising cattle was a side business. Some, like John, had sufficient knowledge and experience to properly manage all the aspects of getting cattle to the market for a profit. There were others who should have invested their funds somewhere else.

That economic climate created an unexpected opportunity for me. It gave me an opening to meet people who owned a few cows and also had pets at home. I found that pet owners were a lot slower to try the new vet with the animals that lived in their house than they were to seek his help with those out in a pasture. The whole situation accelerated the pet side of our practice by allowing me to build trust through treating the large animals first.

As a well-known person in the community, John helped me meet a lot of new clients. He was a talented accountant, too, so he kept the business side of the practice healthy while I was busy keeping animals healthy.

Sadly, John passed away from a massive heart attack at a young age, leaving behind a wife, a son, and two beautiful daughters. In a short time, he made an impact on me, and he is one of those people I will forever remember as a good man and a good friend.

Roberts Realty

"Don't worry; you'll soon be busier than you want to be." On some of those early days when the phone didn't ring and traffic streamed by just yards away from our front door, it was hard to believe those words spoken by Bill and Willa Roberts. Their real estate business shared a wall with us on Main Street.

Theirs was one of the farms I'd visited before "opening day." It was a few miles outside of town, and I showed up early one morning to help with some general herd management. I was nervous, and my anxiety had led to a small conflict with Connie the night before. She loves watching the Academy Awards. That's fine, of course, but they go on and on, way past a reasonable bedtime. There was no place to get out of earshot in our small house, so my attempts to get some sleep only added to my anxiety and frustration. "Does she not understand how big a deal this farm call is tomorrow morning? How can I be my best without enough sleep?" Now, of course, I can see how foolish I was to worry about such a thing when I was only 26 years old!

I arrived at the farm on time and fully prepared to administer Brucellosis vaccine to twenty-five or thirty young heifers. Brucellosis is a devastating disease of breeding cattle capable of wiping out a herd by causing abortions. At the time there was a rigorous government-led eradication program with the goal of getting all 50 states Brucellosis-free. Only a licensed and accredited veterinarian could administer the vaccine. Each female animal receiving the vaccine had to be tagged with an official ear tag and a tattoo placed on the inside of the ear. All the information had to be precisely recorded with a copy sent to the state agency, another given to the owner, and one kept by the attending veterinarian. Adult cattle required testing, and a single positive test meant quarantine of the entire herd, elimination of infected animals, and a series of follow-up tests over several months until the herd was declared Brucellosis-free.

While it's never good to accidentally inject any animal vaccine into a person, the Brucellosis vaccine is particularly dangerous. Accidental injection of Brucellosis vaccine can result in a life-long battle with a disease known as undulant fever in people. I'd heard of several veterinarians who were suffering from such incidents.

Just as we were finishing the vaccinations, Bill announced he had one more patient for me to take a look at before I left. He led me to a small, musty stall where she quietly waited. As the door opened rays of morning sunlight exposed the thick dust floating in the air. I'd come to love the smell of hay mixed with soil inside old wooden structures like this one. My patient began to nervously stir as we led her outside where I'd have enough light to perform a proper examination. The diagnosis came quickly as soon as I could see her udder. She had an advanced case of mastitis and the left rear quarter showed ominous signs of gangrene. Her best option was to prevent the infection from spreading and eventually taking her life.

Clients can take bad news fine as long as you're straightforward and explain the challenges and the plan of action. Bill was okay with the probability of selling this brood cow for beef in a few months after we stopped the infection.

I was happily surprised to realize that the nastier and smellier a case was, the better I liked it. This one fits well into that category as I drained what I could from the udder through a large cannula placed in the orifice at the end of the infected teat. Then I carefully trimmed away dead, purple skin and applied antibiotic ointment after cleaning the wounds with a disinfectant solution. I'd need to return every day for a while until no more dead tissue developed and the affected tissue changed to granulating tissue. By the time we finished all that, she was healthy other than the loss of one of her milk-producing mammary quarters.

Word spread about cases like that one and soon cattle

and dairy farmers in Morgan County began to decide this young animal doctor knew something about veterinary medicine, after all.

My friendship with the Roberts family came with a serendipitous aspect. It turned out Willa was related to Dr. John McCormick. Doctor John was my absolute favorite large animal professor while I was at Auburn, and their relationship gave me a connection back to him. In fact, we had a chance to chat a few minutes when he and Jan came by one day to visit Bill and Willa. Since then he's written books about his experiences as a veterinarian, which is no small encouragement for me to follow suit. Thanks, Dr. McCormick!

Sam Anders

Most people would say ours was a rather odd friendship because of the difference in our ages. Sam Anders was in his late sixties, while I was in my late twenties. But, we fed off each other in a way that was just plain fun. Our friendship grew stronger until his sudden passing from a heart attack on a Sunday morning when he was 75 years old.

Sam lived a few miles outside Hartselle on a farm where he was born. His three sons lived nearby, and each one had his own small cattle farm. It would have been hard to find many people in the area who did not know the Anders family. I was fortunate to work with them for many years.

Sam loved to go to a local restaurant about a half-mile down Highway 31 from PAH. The main draw for him was a gathering of men at what he named "The Liars' Table." Putting the name aside, it was a gathering place for men like the mayor, bankers, and other local business owners.

You could say it was the unofficial chamber of commerce! My being a part of that group was not wasted time even though it kept me out of the office on numerous occasions.

One of the reasons so many people loved Sam Anders was his ability to share his wisdom with pithy one-liners that made everybody laugh out loud. And he loved practical jokes. One spring morning he announced that he'd posted a sign in the local banker's yard saying, "Onions for sale," referring, of course to an overgrowth of those pesky wild onions that show up every year.

I managed to give Sam a dose of his own medicine a couple of times. One came unexpectedly when I was in his barn treating a cow for a retained placenta. The placenta normally falls out immediately after calving, of course, but from time to time that doesn't happen and you can imagine the odor after 3 or 4 days of parts of the placenta hanging out just below the tail. The standard procedure for veterinarians back then was to insert a gloved arm into the reproductive tract and carefully detach and remove the retained parts of the placenta. On this day Sam was standing and sneaking peaks from near the door of the stall. Suddenly he disappeared, and I heard some serious gastric emptying and retching coming from the barn hall. I kidded him pretty hard, but I never mentioned it at The Liars' Table.

On another day he popped into the hospital to get me to go get some coffee just as I was beginning an exam of a small puppy that a client had dropped off. When I removed the rectal thermometer, I couldn't resist the urge to "get him again." I quickly raised my hand with the thermometer to my face and licked my little finger making it appear I'd licked the nasty thermometer. His reaction was predictable!

I'd give a lot for one more trip to The Liars' Table with Sam Anders!

Shirley Russell

Mrs. Russell was one of the first clients to entrust a beloved pet into my care. She came into the tiny office space on Main Street one morning with her calm, healthy Doberman Pincher. As always, she was straightforward, yet pleasant and told me right away she was there because she was tired of taking Inky all the way to Decatur for veterinary care. She'd decided to give the new young vet a try.

I must have done an okay job because she became a long-time client, but I know Connie had a lot to do with it, too. She was still at the front desk working as our receptionist at the time, and the two quickly bonded and chatted endlessly while I examined her pet.

Shirley's sister-in-law, Sandy, soon became a long-term client as well and together they boosted our clientele significantly by encouraging friends to give PAH a try.

For years to come, Connie taught their kids piano lessons at our home. This endeavor not only brought in some extra cash but also helped broaden our reputation in the community. There were lots of connecting factors and people working together to grow Pearson Animal Hospital.

James Stephenson

During the 1970's and 80's, dairy farms were common in North Alabama. James Stephenson was one of the most prominent dairy farm owners. The city of

Hartselle had grown over the years so that his farm was barely outside the city limits by the time I arrived.

I particularly enjoyed working with Mr. Stephenson and his two sons because they ran such an efficient operation. When they called me, it was always for a particular need such as a cow with a foot problem, or they needed me to perform some herd work like testing for Brucellosis.

Like all efficient dairy farmers, the Stephenson men knew how to perform a lot of medical care themselves. They also recognized when veterinary assistance was in order. One such time involved a heavily producing cow with a case of persistent mastitis. They'd treated her with over-the-counter udder infusions of antibiotics, but none had worked so far. They called me out to check on her condition.

We discussed our options, which included sending a sample to the lab for culture and sensitivity. We decided to try a new antibiotic infusion, which was available only through veterinarians. I was aware of the product because of a recent conversation with a sales representative from the Upjohn Company. The idea of a salesman may not carry a positive connotation for a lot of folks, but I found them to be an invaluable source of up-to-date information. I could get continuing education on a regular basis right there in my exam room by listening to those guys.

What I'd learned from Warren Barton, the Upjohn representative, aided my practice because I'd trusted him enough to go ahead and order some of the new mastitis tubes.

We carefully infused the medication, and I left enough for treatments the following two days. It sure was good to get that phone call saying the infusions led to a cure.

Gene "Big Deal" Eason

Dairy farmers turned out to be a close-knit group, so it wasn't long until word spread, and I found myself visiting several dairies in the area. One of those occupied a peaceful spot of land in what's known as Cedar Cove. It was a huge horseshoe-shaped tract of farmland outlined by a dirt road about five miles long. It was always good to get called to Mr. Gene Eason's farm because a trip out to Cedar Cove was almost like a trip to the Great Smoky Mountains. The tall, hardwood trees on the mountains that surround the cove are beautiful in every season of the year.

Dairymen seem to develop a sixth sense about calling for professional help when one of their valuable cows is about to "freshen." That expression refers to when a cow gives birth, and it comes from the fact that it marks the beginning of a new term of milk production.

So when Mr. Eason called saying one of his cows needed my assistance in calving, I knew not to delay. Hurrying to pull on my coveralls and rubber boots, I was met at the door by a thin young girl with short dark hair who wouldn't let me out until she let me know she was there for a job interview. I needed to hire someone to be "all everything" because Connie had fought morning sickness as long as she could. I took one look at Vicky, and something told me she would fit the need. So, on the way out the door, I declared, "You got the job. Be here at 8 o'clock in the morning."

I've always wished someone could have been with me on that cold February morning at the Eason Dairy. Delivering calves is a fulfilling activity because it's one of those times when your work benefits a cow in trouble, an anxious owner, and, of course, a new life trying to enter the world. Only this time there were two new lives wrapped up inside this Holstein. The black nose barely protruding from the vulva convinced me the problem was an abnormal presentation where the front legs stretch out behind the head, and the resulting mass is too large to come through the birth canal. A few minutes of pushing the head back and repositioning the front legs to the normal presentation allowed for progress to begin. Assuming this was an oversized calf, I applied gobs of lubricant to the head and finally made the delivery. What I saw was both dramatic and heartbreaking. I had just delivered my first and only two-headed calf.

Before you jump to conclusions, the second head was not complete or separate. Instead, it consisted of an eye, ear, and partial mouth, which attached near the jaw. The little fellow only took a few breaths before expiring, so I'm sure there were other life-threatening defects, which were less apparent. His "twin sister" was healthy and survived just fine.

The Ward Family

Across the cove on the south side of the horseshoe lay a large farm owned by the Ward family. There were two brothers, Wayne and Russell and three sisters, Faye, Louise, and Barbara.

The two brothers along with two brothers-in-law, Dwayne and Phillip, kept the farm running with a high degree of efficiency while they each worked a "day job" off the farm. The land was flat and very fertile. As a result, several cuttings of nutritious hay rested in huge round bales across the landscape.

Almost every time I came home from a trip to Cedar Cove, I'd comment to Connie how nice it would be to live out there. Our dreaming finally got serious enough that Connie convinced me to call Russell (aka, Tommy in the family) and ask if they'd consider selling us some acreage to build a house. A few months later we were living in our dream home at the foot of a mountain in the midst of the Ward family of Cedar Cove. The next 14 years were some of the best of our lives. So good in fact, they'd support another book writing!

Beverly Waldrop

Beverly taught school at F. E. Burleson Elementary. I'm sure her students benefited from her calm, assuring demeanor and voice. Her Sheltie named "Puppy" benefitted as well. He was one of our calmest and most pleasant patients. He never missed an appointment for exams and vaccinations of for annual teeth cleaning. Every time we saw him, his long thick fur was brushed as though heading to a dog show.

Beverly was among the teachers who invited me to speak to young students at the school every year about what it's like to be a veterinarian. I hope the kids enjoyed it as much as I did. I'm sure the time invested in school rooms added support to our practice.

First Baptist Church

Honestly, I was reluctant to join the First Baptist Church (FBC) because I knew it could appear as a business decision more than a spiritual one. But Earl Cook and a few other members insisted we at least give them a try. We did join there, and it was a spiritual decision because Connie and I both sensed God's pleasure with our choice.

The years that followed confirmed what we sensed in powerful ways. We grew spiritually, we found opportunities to serve, and we made lifelong friendships in the congregation.

There are rewards associated with church membership that must be experienced to understand, let alone appreciate. If your mother always loved you, no matter what, then you have an idea of the positive side of church membership. We've always felt unconditional love from the folks at FBC in Hartselle even though we moved away many years ago.

Still, there is probably no single factor which stimulated the growth of PAH more than FBC Hartselle. People with all kinds of animals, large and small, flooded our practice, and they came with amiable and supportive attitudes.

In all my years of practice in which I spayed and neutered thousands of animals, only two female cats continued having estrus after the surgery. Each of those belonged to a couple of preachers! It was quite embarrassing for me, but the preachers took it in stride and didn't seem to lose confidence in my abilities as a veterinary surgeon.

This condition can occur as a result of either the presence of abnormal ovarian tissue or because of incomplete removal of normal ovaries at the time of surgery. Neither owner wanted follow-up surgery to look for and remove any remaining ovaries, so I never knew which it was in those cats.

4 FUN PET NAMES

A heart of peace gives life to the body.
Proverbs 14:30

On many occasions, practicing veterinary medicine is a potent producer of stress for everyone involved. Anything that engenders a smile in the midst of the tension is always welcome. Sometimes pet names can create an involuntary smile on even the most stressed of faces. This power becomes significant when combined with the appearance or personality displayed by the pet or, in some cases, the owner of the pet. And, yes, it's remarkable how often pets look like their people.

My all-time favorite was a coonhound named **Evinrude**. Let me help you make the connection. The owner of this dog was particularly proud of the speed with which his raccoon-hunting dog could swim across streams in pursuit of his nocturnal target. Of course, Evinrude is a popular model marine outboard motor.

Humper was a tiny, undeniably ugly little mixed-breed dog with stringy black hair. If ever a dog needed orthodontic braces, it was *Humper*. But, his owner was a macho type guy who apparently wanted to convey that looks can be deceiving.

Zeus was by far the most massive Great Dane I've ever seen. I don't know how much he weighed because he refused to stand on the floor scales at our hospital throughout his whole life. In fact, pushing him toward the scales was the only thing that brought a hint of aggression from that gentle giant. Without a doubt, he would have topped 200 pounds. Zeus was like his owner in that he was tall and muscular and not overweight.

Bear is a common pet name most anywhere in the nation, I'm sure. But in the state of Alabama, more often than not, it was a reference to the former football coach in Tuscaloosa. Those miniature Poodles, Chihuahuas, and Yorkshire Terriers named Bear were especially entertaining to Auburn fans like me.

Paddle Foot was an oversized yellow tabby cat born with extra toes on all his feet. This frisky feline with long, thick hair had few enemies. All aggressors quickly learned the power of those extra claws. No, we didn't charge an additional fee for the declaw procedure when his owner tired of replacing scratched up furniture.

I remember with clarity when a childhood friend came in with her son and his two male cats named **Tubal and Jubal**. I was a little embarrassed when I asked where he'd come up with names for the male siblings. I was humbled when he told me they were biblical names. A little biblical investigation that night enlightened me about these characters mentioned in Genesis 4.

Fiona is a somewhat enigmatic name in my

estimation since there are so few people to identify with it. Why name this average looking, medium-size, mixed-breed, brownish dog Fiona? It seemed to be related to the personality of the owner who was interestingly mysterious, too.

Next, I have to mention several pet names derived from TV and movie characters. Here's a list of a few of the most popular names.

- Mr. Spock
- Mr. T
- Elvis
- Goober
- Chewbacca
- Rambo
- Boba Fett
- Linus
- Paddington
- Starsky
- Hutch

Those "celebrity" names often put me at a disadvantage when meeting pets for the first time. I've never been a big fan of TV shows or movies, which meant I had no idea how to make a connection to the character and react appropriately.

I met **Floorboard** during a rabies vaccination clinic on a hot summer day. He was a Blue Tick Hound. Treating hounds is almost always enjoyable because of their laid-back disposition. Floorboard was literally laid back below the glove compartment when we met.

Most of the time, people at rabies clinics get their pets out of their vehicle and stand in line to register and get tags and certificates of vaccination. That sped up the process considerably because it allowed me to walk along giving the injections while the owners restrained the patients.

But, there was a good reason for Floorboard's name. The floorboard in front of the passenger seat was where he always lay for trips of every kind. Once there, he was totally averse to getting out before arriving back to his home and familiar surroundings.

Smart veterinarians know the importance of restraint and positioning when sticking a sharp needle into an animal. Of course, Floorboard didn't care about any of that stuff. Plus, his owner went on and on about how harmless old Floorboard had always been around folks. "Why, he wouldn't bite a biscuit, Doc."

There's just something about a bargain that makes people get in a hurry. I guess it's that old emotion called, "Fear of Missing Out." Floorboard's owner must have been thinking we'd go on to the next stop on our route before he could get that old hound to climb out of his comfort zone. And if that happened, he'd have to make a trip into town where the fee would be a whole dollar more for the same vaccination.

With visions of a crowded parking lot already waiting at the next stop, I decided to reach in and trustingly give the injection as painlessly as possible. I knew I didn't want to get to the next stop late and have to hear a burning up, snuff dipping farmer in overalls and long sleeve shirt say, "Doc, we uz 'bout to leave cuz it looked like you forgot 'bout us here in the Ebenezer community."

The good news is, old Floorboard lived up to his reputation and never flinched while I pulled up his loose skin and slipped the needle in and infused the subcutaneous vaccine. The bad news is, it convinced me I could get away with it on the next patient in the floorboard of a pickup truck. You'll hear more about that later.

Bama has to be the most common name for pets in our state. I've encountered snakes, turtles, guinea pigs and a raccoon carrying that name. But usually, it's given to dogs and sometimes to horses.

The most fun I ever had with a pet named Bama involved a shaggy old Chow dog. He lived on a farm and never got the hair brushing he desperately needed.

So, from time to time his owner brought him to us for a haircut. We didn't perform grooming services, so this was always sort of a salvage procedure. The mats were always thick and mixed with dirt, leaves, and twigs. Plus, there was no space between the skin and the mats, which meant a complete shaving was the only option.

We decided Bama needed to retain at least a little of his red fur to avoid weeks of complete nakedness. So, we left his hair long over the last five inches of his tail and around his head.

Mr. Eddy almost refused to take him home that afternoon saying he was now a lion and not a dog.

5 SEVEN INTERESTING AND INSPIRING CLIENTS

Whoever is righteous has regard for the life of his animal. Proverbs 12:10

I've mentioned **Mrs. Andre Reed** before because she was my first and last client to see for an appointment during my time at PAH. But, there's much to tell about her character during the between years.

I believe I did some of my best work for Mrs. Reed. Why? It was because I knew she trusted me as her veterinarian. I realize that all of our long-term clients believed in me, but Mrs. Reed somehow made me feel that trust with every interaction we had in the client-patient-doctor relationship.

One of the toughest challenges faced by veterinarians is what's called "client compliance." By that, we mean getting clients actually to follow through on your recommendations. It's always been baffling to me that people take the time and invest the cash into veterinary visits, then go home and fail to follow directions. We know this from getting responses on later visits after prescribing an antibiotic and the client says, "Oh, I still have plenty of those from the last time." No wonder you're back for the same problem! And no wonder pathogens keep developing resistance to antibiotics.

Mrs. Reed was the pleasant exception to this malady. This widowed Mom who worked long hours as a nurse at the local hospital managed to finish whatever meds we prescribed for her pets. Her motivation? She loved her pets, and she trusted us to help her take good care of them.

It's a wonder I didn't slip up and refer to **Mrs. Robbie Stephenson** as "Aunt Robbie." She's just one of those people who makes you feel as though you are her favorite nephew.

Her husband, Robert, served Hartselle as mayor for several years. Their small farm was one of many that'd been swallowed up by the expanding city limits. We became friends while I helped care for their cows, dogs, and cats.

There was an incident involving one of their Basset hounds that I'll never forget. Bassets have big brown eyes that are so lovable they make it easy to overlook the prominent ears hanging on the side of their heads. The Stephensons owned multiple Bassets and one of their favorites managed to break off one of his canine teeth. That's the long, fang-like tooth near the front of the mouth.
Because pain in the broken tooth caused him to eat less and begin losing weight, we decided to extract the offending tooth. If I could go back, I'd refer that patient to

the vet school at Auburn. But, even though adult canine teeth have incredibly long roots, I knew it was within my ability to perform the surgery. And, yes, we did successfully extract the entire tooth, root and all.

As I was suturing the gum tissue over the space left by the root of the tooth, the bleeding seemed a little excessive, even after applying pressure for a while using gauze sponges. Finally, after inserting a clotting material into the cavity and placing tight sutures across it, the bleeding seemed to be under control.

Unfortunately, he still didn't make it.

It bothers me that I'll never know for sure, but it seems likely that he carried some inherited clotting disorder such as Von Willebrand disease. I'm sure we could have detected it before extracting the tooth by sending a blood sample to a specialized lab, but I hadn't seen any indication that he may have had the condition.

I'm also sure that losing that pet caused Mrs. Stephenson and her family to experience a deep sense of loss. But, as you might imagine, she was very gracious about it and assured me she knew I'd tried to do the right thing. Clients like her are what enable veterinarians to keep on practicing and learning.

Mr. Frank Stewart owned the local *Western Auto Store*. He had a personality and demeanor that just made you feel good about yourself and life in general. Apparently, lots of folks sensed the same thing because his business was one of the most successful in Hartselle.

Mr. Stewart and I had more than animals in common. Being loyal fans of Auburn football always gave us plenty to talk about, even during some lean years for the Tigers.

Because I was running a business, I learned a lot from shopping in his store and observing his interaction with customers who came in while I was there. He managed to get each shopper into a conversation about something they had in common. I believe he spent most of his time talking about stuff unrelated to anything his store had to sell. He understood his customers were interested in things like football, farming, Christmas parades, and general "Hartselle stuff." I'm confident he had a host of loyal customers.

Before long we discovered we had another common interest. His son, Barry, went to Auburn and earned his degree in veterinary medicine. Lots of conversations followed about how Barry was doing in school and how proud he was of him. I knew I'd be gaining a valuable colleague when he graduated. It turns out; I was right about that.

Soon after graduation, Dr. Barry Stewart and I discussed the possibility of working together at PAH. We would have made a substantial partnership because we respected each other, and our personalities and different skills would have complimented each other very well. But, his dream was to own a practice in his hometown eventually. And because his Dad instilled honesty and integrity into Barry, he made that clear up front. It seemed too risky for me at the time, so we decided he would not work at PAH again, now that he had his degree.

By the way, PAH and HAC (Hartselle Animal Clinic) are still thriving, serving Morgan County, and providing jobs and livelihoods for families. And we still have an excellent relationship.

Mrs. Pat Patillo represents a class of clients typical

of all veterinary practices. But, in all other ways, she was in a class all her own.

She was one of those clients who came to our animal hospital for social interaction as much as for medical assistance. She never showed up without her full complement of makeup, proper dress, and flamboyant personality.

Quite often her husband, Hugh, came along, too. Better known as "Pat," the distinguished colonel and West Point graduate served with the US Army in Korea and Vietnam. His brother, Ralph, made the ultimate sacrifice in 1971 while serving in Vietnam. Mrs. Pat and Colonel Pat often spoke of him because he was listed as MIA for years before being presumed dead. It was a tragedy that weighed heavily on both of them as long as I knew them.

Nobody ever took better care of their pets than the Patillos. One of their Dachshunds got into some rat poison once, and she rushed frantically into the hospital with a mix of anxiety and guilt. I assured her we could take care of the problem since she'd brought him in soon after he ate the toxic pellets. Wouldn't you just know, that dog resisted regurgitating his stomach contents until after the third dose of oral hydrogen peroxide? Mrs. Patillo had about worried herself sick by that time.

They were loyal clients who made a significant contribution to the euphoric experience of serving clients in Hartselle, Alabama, in those days.

I did not grow up on a farm. In fact, I lived in a neighborhood in Decatur, Alabama. My only exposure to farm animals consisted of occasional visits to one uncle who ran a laying hen operation and another uncle who raised show horses. Because I suffered from asthma as a child, I was never able to be in dusty environments. Praise the Lord I outgrew asthma long before making farm calls.

It took only a short time to appreciate the good-natured character of cattle farmers. Almost all of them I encountered proved to be honest, hardworking, and pleasant clients. Although I never gave it much thought then, surely all of them could quickly detect that my background was different than theirs. Somehow, they accepted me and trusted me to care for the animals that provided significant income for their families.

So, it's incredible that I had the good fortune to get to know **Mr. John Knight** who raised polled Hereford cattle in Lacon, Alabama.

It's hard to put into words how inspirational Mr. Knight was to me. His impact involved a lot more than the fact that he reminded me of my Granddaddy Pearson. Both men were small in stature and spoke sparingly with quiet voices. Both of them served as deacons in their church, and both earned the respect of their families and acquaintances. Both were successful owners of a small business.

Every spring for many years Mr. Knight, his son, and grandson herded all the cattle into a corral and hired me to perform annual deworming, vaccinating, and testing. They were always super-organized and knowledgeable and made me look good. Many times during the rest of the year, I'd get a smile on my face when I got to make a call to that farm in southern Morgan County.

During the hot summer months, he'd frequently call me to his farm to treat several calves suffering from a condition called "pinkeye." My services were economically important because the pain and loss of sight significantly affected overall health.

Because a bacterium causes the condition, subconjunctival injections were highly effective. Back then, the FDA still allowed an injectable made up of three drugs: penicillin, streptomycin, and a corticosteroid.

On lots of occasions, after we finished treating the cattle, Mr. Knight would slip on a pair of work gloves and ease into the barn for a minute or two. He had a unique way with animals large and small. I never noticed any frustration or urgency in his voice nor any squealing from the two or three cats he retrieved for a rabies vaccination.

The hood of my truck served as the treatment table for the injections. Once the cats were set free to scurry back to the barn, that same hood morphed into a sort of desk where he'd write checks for my services. Notice I said, "Checks." The option of payment that seemed routine and unremarkable to him demonstrated a rare level of integrity to me.

He always wrote one check for the cattle treatments, which was tax deductible. Then another one for the cat vaccinations, which are not. Most people would feel comfortable just lumping it all together. After all, those cats served a purpose by controlling losses from mice eating into feeds.

But not Mr. John Knight. He always made an effort to maintain his integrity. My Granddaddy was like that, too. I'm thankful I knew both of them, and I hope I can live up to their examples in my own life.

Mr. and Mrs. C.W. Craze lived in a modest home alongside Highway 36 West about halfway between

Hartselle and Danville, Alabama. Although the dwelling with yellow shingle siding often went unnoticed by travelers on the busy highway, it was always kept clean, neat, and attractive by its occupants. The inside of the home was as appealing as the outside.

A visit to this farm was always an uplifting experience. Most of the calls I made there were to deliver a large, healthy calf. C.W. and Louise would not allow any prolonged suffering due to a problematic birth, so the outcome could reasonably be expected to be a live birth.

But there was a lot more to it than that. I never saw this couple in a bad mood. Instead, they always greeted me with big smiles and laughter. There was never any need to chase a patient across a pasture, through woods, or fishponds. They consistently had the patient confined to a barn or at least in a loading chute by the time I arrived.

However, there was one time I thought I would freeze to death. It was mid-morning on a bright, windy and cold January day. This time the patient was in a chute in the open pasture instead of inside the barn. The profuse apologies coming from the Crazes warmed my heart but didn't do much for my exposed torso, nose, and ears.

Because of the high humidity in Alabama, cold, windy weather can chill you to the bone. I don't even like the cold air in the freezer section of a grocery store. So I had to grit my teeth and hold my breath as I stripped down to short-sleeved coveralls and pulled on thin plastic shoulder length gloves. Regardless of the temperature, that's necessary attire for delivering a calf.

After applying plenty of lubricant to my arms, the confines of the birth canal afforded comforting warmth. That's why in times like this you switch arms often. In this case, I was happy to find the cause of the dystocia. Although the nose of the calf was entering the birth canal, both front legs were behind the head.

While my left arm was in up to my shoulder, it enjoyed the return of circulation and a soothing feeling of warmth on a cold day. However, the right arm and hand negated the euphoria by getting colder and colder. Of course, the opposite was true after one leg fell into place and the process began with my right arm inside.

Fortunately, once the calf was worked into position, delivery came easy by applying pressure and pulling the feet at the same time the cow had a contraction. Soon there was a large, wide-eyed heifer looking around as though to say, "Where am I?" All I needed to do then was back away, let Momma lick her newborn, and see how fast I could get a coat on and get into the truck!

Back in the truck, Mr. Craze was going on from the passenger seat about how he appreciated me coming out and helping him on such a cold morning. Before we arrived at the house, he insisted I come inside to warm up and wash my hands. Mrs. Craze had a hot cup of coffee ready on the kitchen table along with the farm checkbook. Even though I realized there was work waiting for me back at the office, I'm glad I took some extra time for conversation with good friends who happened to be clients.

By August of that first year in Hartselle, my level of confidence had risen to a fairly comfortable level. After all, I'd been practicing on my own since March. Still, veterinarians always have in the back of their mind the fact that any day can bring a challenge big enough to test their confidence and skills.

The ringing phone woke me up from one of those deep Sunday afternoon naps. I'm not sure how I sounded when I answered, but the person on the other end conveyed urgency and concern. It was my first introduction to **Julie Johnston** who was frantic to get some help for her pony who was in labor but not making much progress. It was immediately apparent, even on the phone, that this person cared deeply for her animal.

The oppressive August heat caught my attention as I climbed into the truck and cranked the engine. Sure, Alabama has days that are neither hot and humid or windy and cold. But farm calls seem to come rarely on "normal" days.

It was a short drive from my house to the Johnston farm located just inside the city limits on Thompson Road. As I drove into the driveway, my eyes gazed at the beautiful setting. The two-story white house sat atop a gentle rise behind a white picket fence. To top it off, I noticed a pond halfway between the home and the road. Among my thoughts was the dream of one day living in a similar setting.

Julie was in the pasture near the road brushing her beloved pony. Her body language reminded me of nervous fathers I'd seen portrayed on TV shows like *Gunsmoke* when their wives were in labor.

Here's why I mentioned the confidence and skill subject: That day would be my first time to assist an equine dystocia. Never in vet school or during a year working at Bentley Animal Hospital had I even observed an assisted equine birth. I did know enough to be cautious of the delicate tissues in the birth canal of this patient. I knew there would be drastic consequences if a tear developed between the birth canal and colon, which lie precariously near each other. Those are concerns with cattle, too. But bovine tissue is much sturdier and less likely to tear.

I wondered if Julie attributed the sweat pouring off my head to the heat instead of my level of anxiety. I did learn something valuable that day about Julie and her parents. They were trusting and supportive of whatever I did or recommended. You can quickly detect when a client has doubts about your ability. Some folks are just that way. The Johnstons were the kind of clients I was hoping to find.

Hopefully, you've picked up on the fact that I give God credit for any success I enjoyed while practicing veterinary medicine. Indeed, this was one of those times He blessed me with a successful delivery. No damage resulted to that small pony or her foal, and a long-term relationship was born between Pearson Animal Hospital and the Johnston family.

6 CHALLENGING CASES

Do not be afraid of sudden terror or of the ruin of the wicked, when it comes, for the Lord will be your confidence and will keep your foot from being caught. Proverbs 3:2

Corn cob hound

We were still in the three-room business complex on Main Street when I first met Danny McKleskey. I have to admit, I have an affinity for large dogs. It's not that I dislike smaller ones; I just enjoy the large ones.

Danny showed up one morning with a Bluetick Hound who obviously felt terrible. His head was down, his tail was droopy, and a string of saliva hung from his lips. His normally voracious appetite was gone, and he'd vomited every time he drank water. Palpation of the abdomen revealed a relatively large, firm mass.

Placing him on the floor, we made abdominal x-rays and then developed them on the exam table in the middle room using aluminum cooking pans to hold the chemicals. It was easy to view the mass, but all we could tell was that it was not anything very dense like bone or metal. The course of action was clear. Danny's prize hound needed exploratory surgery.

Although the building we were practicing in was small, and not designed to house a veterinary hospital, I purchased proper equipment from the very beginning. So, we were able to assess kidney, liver, and pancreatic function of surgical patients before anesthetizing them.

Not many years before, intravenous sodium pentobarbital was the most commonly used anesthetic for animals. Besides being dangerous because the narrow range between adequate and overdose was small, patients often remained in a stupor for up to three days following surgery.

Thankfully, when our practice opened, we were able to use methoxyflurane, which is a form of gas anesthesia. It was incredibly safer because it allowed control of anesthetic depth and reduced recovery time down to an hour or less.

But back to Danny's Bluetick Hound. We discovered that he'd taken a liking to corncobs. Apparently he liked them so much, he swallowed one almost intact. Naturally, it became hopelessly lodged as it passed through his stomach into the small intestines.

Being the excellent dog breeder he was, Danny had sought our help quickly, and little or no tissue damage had occurred. We were able to find the problem and remove the cob. Because the kernels were gone, it wouldn't have been long before the rough surface attached to the intestinal lining and caused a lot of tissue destruction.

Mosquitoes don't like cow insides.

One of the most fun perks of practicing veterinary medicine is getting to learn natural phenomena while working through a typical day.

When Waymon came into the office late one afternoon in July, he was his usual soft-spoken, relaxed self. I suspect that if he'd gone to the fire department to report a blaze, he'd still be calm and unperturbed.

Like so many of our clients, he worked all day at a plant in Decatur and checked his cattle when he got home. He informed me on this day how he'd found a heifer in labor and it didn't look like she'd be able to deliver her calf. Nothing unusual about that, right? So, I followed him out to his farm and patiently waited as he opened the barbed wire gate to the pasture. I could see my patient lying beside a small pond, bowing her back and straining with tail raised. Nothing was making it to the outside of the birth canal.

As I exited the truck and started preparations for my initial examination, my concentration was interrupted by a swarm of dive-bombing, aggressive mosquitoes. After a short appraisal of the situation within the pelvic cavity, two things became apparent. First, having a combination of blood and placental fluids on my gloved hands significantly restricted my ability to shew away mosquitoes from my face. On a larger scale, it was also clear that this mother-to-be was going to require a C-section for delivery.

All during the preparation of the surgical site and placement of local anesthesia, those pesky mosquitoes intensified their attack as the sun began its descent toward the horizon. There just wasn't much we could do except work as rapidly as possible and try to ignore the itchy spots on our necks and noses.

But as soon as I completed the incision and the odor from inside that bovine permeated the air, we both noticed the mosquitoes had disappeared.

When I drove away glancing at the rearview mirror reflecting a new calf nursing, I thought how lucky I was to witness two miracles on one summer afternoon. The thought of getting rich by discovering a new, highly efficient insect repellant soon faded away when the next busy day dawned and filled my time with far more practical matters.

A severed jugular vein

I've never seen a more relaxed presentation of a medical emergency than the owner who placed his 9-pound mixed-breed dog onto my exam table and showed me the puncture wounds in her neck (the dog's, that is).

The little black, fuzzy pet was just as unconcerned. No panting or whining. Just looking up at me with no more apprehension than if she'd been at home on the couch.

But a close look at the skin on the left side of her neck revealed a lot more than I expected. The three or four puncture wounds were apparently the result of a big-dog-little-dog fight. In the days when most dogs lived outdoors, those encounters were quite frequent, but the damage left by this one was anything but ordinary.

The surprise was the severed end of the jugular vein protruding through the tear. Amazingly, the hole was small enough to pinch the vessel and prevent leakage, and it was the proximal end of the vein that was sticking out. Otherwise, fatal blood loss would have come quickly as the severed vein tried to transport blood back to the heart.

Knowing that I was no vascular surgeon, I decided to tie off the free end of the vein and treat the wounds routinely. The jugular vein on the opposite side was sufficient to keep circulation going until collateral veins had time to grow in the area. I'm sure that lucky dog never missed a meal or even a treat that day.

Boxer meets bush hog.

Our home was always close enough to the hospital to allow me to go there for lunch (at least on days when we got a lunch break). Doing so served me well by giving me a break and time to unwind in the middle of the day.

On many of those days, the phone was ringing when I walked in the back door of the house. This time it was Vicky frantically saying that Mrs. Gee was on her way in with a Boxer that had gotten too close to a bush hog. It turned out, "BJ" belonged to a neighbor. She knew the injuries were too extensive for most people to try to save his life, so she took him in and made the commitment of nursing him back to health.

Everyone is familiar with the distinct smell of a wet dog, of course. Well, large amounts of blood on the coat of dogs creates its distinctive odor. Once you've experienced it, you always recognize it anytime and anywhere. That was the scent that greeted me all the way at the back entrance that day.

Blood was still oozing from the makeshift pillowcase bandage wrapped tightly around the right front paw. I was dismayed to see the same situation on his right rear paw,

49

too. Blood poured from numerous severed vessels, but the bandages had slowed the bleeding down enough to prevent hypovolemic shock. Using a tourniquet above each foot, we removed the bandage to observe the extent of the damage.

Amputation was the only option for the front limb. Amputation had to be considered for the rear leg as well because of the four compound fractures left behind from the encounter with a whirling mower blade. By definition, a compound fracture is one in which part of the broken bone is protruding through the skin. Poor BJ had four compound fractures involving each large metatarsal bone. Those are the long bones between the ankle and toes of a person.

Adding to the challenge was the loss of a significant amount of skin and tissue around the broken bones.

After consulting with Mrs. Gee, we decided to try and save the rear leg. We had plenty of stainless steel intramedullary pins pre-autoclaved, and by that time I had enough experience with them to stabilize the bones.

So we took BJ to surgery and one-by-one reduced each fracture by placing pins into each bone. The thorough cleansing of the wounds and the antibiotic injections kept infection down. Bandages had to be changed daily for quite a while until tissue granulated around and closed the wounds.

BJ came back for check-ups for years afterward, and unless you looked at the scars on that paw, you'd never know anything had happened.

When BJ had lived his full life, Mr. and Mrs. Gee wanted to have his remains cremated. That's a procedure much less common back then that it is now. They took his body to Dr. Bentley in Huntsville who had one of the only crematories in Alabama at the time. Years later when Mr. Gee passed away, BJ's remains were buried with him.

A "really big" reason to spay your dog.

Over the years we saw numerous cases similar to the one I'm about to describe. But this first one seen during the first year of PAH was particularly interesting because it was the first time my assistants, Vicky and Kathy, had ever seen one like it. Plus, it turned out to possibly have the highest size-to-dog ratio of any I've ever seen.

The patient presented as a 37-pound mix-breed female dog. She was thin, except for her huge, prominent potbelly. Her orange, unhealthy hair coat matched her sickly body language and slightly sunken eyes.

The diagnosis of pyometra came quickly since this was what's classified as an open pyometra (i.e., a uterine infection). That means a small stream of pus was dripping from her backside. When a patient has a closed pyometra, there is no drainage to observe, and the diagnosis requires more investigation. Plus, those are even more dangerous to the dog.

Because the emergency condition is an entire uterus filled with pus, the treatment is surgical removal of the infected uterus and the ovaries. In other words, a "complicated spay" must be performed as soon as possible.

That's exactly what we did that morning. I always enjoyed these surgeries because there was no doubt that it was a life-saving procedure. In most cases, dramatic improvement is evident within a few hours after surgery.

As I mentioned, this was the first of many pyometra cases for Vicky and Kathy to assist with and observe. Their wide-eyed expressions divulged their disbelief as the huge, doughy organ was pulled up through the abdominal incision and laid out onto the surgical drape.

As soon as the procedure was complete, and the menacing, y-shaped uterus was lying free on a counter, Vicky cried out, "Doc, we've got to see how much that thing weighs!" I'm so glad she did because that engorged sack of nasty fluid weighed 13 pounds.

If my math is right, that's 35% of the patient's weight! I was never sure if the owner could appreciate the magnitude of that ratio. But I do know she was happy to take a skinny pet back home!

How'd that stick get in there?

He was a happy-go-lucky, 65 pound black Labrador Retriever and member of his family. His owner brought him to us to find out what was the cause for the hard knot on the side of his neck. As he led his pet into the exam room, he said, "Doc, that thing's been there a while. We've just been really busy lately."

I'm sure my face gave away my perplexity as I ran my fingers across the bulge underneath the skin. The firmness suggested a bone, but there should be no bone between the cervical spine and the trachea. Plus, with a moderate amount of pressure, the object could be moved slightly from side to side.

It didn't take long to realize the only logical course of action was to make an incision directly over the mysterious "bone" for some exploration. After some heavy sedation and local anesthesia, that's what we did.

What appeared was not on the list of possibilities that my mind had imagined. The rounded end of a portion of a wooden stick soon popped out through the skin. It was apparent that it was not going to be a very short stick. And there was no way to determine exactly where the other end lay.

So, I gently but firmly pulled on it until the entire six-inch piece of wood was free and in my hand. I'm sure I held my breath, but there was no change in the breathing of my patient. No coughing, gagging, or wheezing ensued. The wound was flushed out, cleansed, and closed with sutures.

The longer we gazed at the stick, the more puzzled we became. That stick was a part of a tree limb about one-half to three-quarter inches thick and six inches long. The bark was gone entirely, revealing the light yellow wood, with rounded tips on both ends.

I've thought about that incident many times over the years, trying to find a definitive answer as to how that limb got to where it was that day.

The best conclusion I can offer is that this was a typical Lab who'd decided to chew on a tree limb. After working on it until the bark was gone, and he'd enjoyed it until the ends were smooth, he apparently decided to swallow it.

There is an area just behind and between the soft palate and tongue called the oropharynx. The epiglottis directs food toward the esophagus or opens to allow air into the trachea and travel into the lungs. If the stick had gone into the esophagus, those busy owners would have been in a lot sooner with a sick and vomiting dog caused by a blockage in the stomach or intestines.

Apparently, the stake made its way between the small bones of the larynx, passed through a tiny area called a lateral ventricle, on into the soft tissue of the neck without causing a lot of pain. Just a splinter or two could have impeded the movement and provoked some desperate breathing problems.

That indiscriminate canine never seemed to be aware of anything out of the ordinary, but he sure provided some fascinating memories for his family and us.

Help! My dog's been shot!

One of the few things that is consistent about practicing veterinary medicine is that Saturday mornings are crazy busy. And that busyness is never more intense than during the summer months.

Right in the middle of one of those busy summer Saturdays, a client came flying through the front door screaming for help. The fact that he'd accidentally shot his Doberman while aiming at a coyote chasing his calves made him even more frantic.

The .223 Remington bullet left a deceptively small tear in the skin between the last two ribs where it entered and a similar wound on the opposite side where it exited at an angle a little farther behind the ribs.

The lack of respiratory distress gave us hope that the lungs weren't damaged, but the pale gums and position of the wounds offered plenty of reason to indicate internal bleeding was actively occurring.

While the receptionist explained the situation to other clients who'd come in that morning for routine medical needs, we quickly induced anesthesia and began an exploratory surgery. After siphoning some blood from the abdomen, a large tear emerged in one lobe of the liver. Livers are wonderful organs with numerous life-supporting functions, and thankfully, large enough to function minus one lobe.

For the first time in my life, I was in the middle of what's technically called a hepatic lobectomy. Somehow I dissected down to where that damaged and bleeding lobe connected to the rest of the liver. Once there, I tied off vessels and tissue and lifted the now useless, purplish-brown glob free and laid it aside.

Finally, there was time to take fresh blood from a large dog the local dog pound loaned us, and the warm red fluid quickly produced some pink color in our patient's gums.

While I returned to an exam room to see a few patiently waiting clients and their pets, one of our nurses stayed close by the recovering Doberman. Incredibly, when she stepped out for just a few seconds, that Doberman suddenly sat up, tried to stand, and immediately fell hard onto the floor.

Although we all looked on in complete disbelief, expecting the worst, no complications ever developed from the short flight from tabletop to the floor. Thankfully, Dobie made many non-emergency visits over the next few years.

7 FUNNY AND EMBARRASSING
EVENTS

This is the day that the LORD has made; let us
rejoice and be glad in it. Psalm 118:24

Our mouths were filled with laughter, our tongues
with songs of joy. Then it was said among the
nations, "The Lord has done great things for them."
Psalm 126:2

The day I met Dr. Will Crouch.

My first year of solo practice began in March of 1973.
Easter was late that year, not showing up on the calendar
until April 22nd. In Alabama, the weather stays on the cold
side right up until Easter, no matter whether it arrives in
March or April. In 1973, as usual, some days during the
weeks right before the holiday were nice and warm.

It was on one such day about mid-April when I was called to assist a cow in labor a few miles out Highway 36 West. When I found the farm, the farmer clad in well-worn coveralls and a ragged University of Alabama cap motioned for me to follow him on his equally well-worn John Deere tractor.

As soon as the distressed bovine spotted my unfamiliar, red and white 1962 Chevrolet pickup truck, she decided to make a getaway by splashing into the pond. Before she stopped, cold, muddy water had submerged half her body and was lapping just below the birth canal.

I reacted like any 25-year-old brand new veterinary practice owner would respond. Besides, it's impressive what actions a combination of low funds in a bank account, impending financial obligations, a pregnant wife, and youthful exuberance can create.

Without giving it much thought, I grabbed my lariat and headed straight into the pond, slowing down long enough to remove my rubber boots. I still don't know what caused me to go in barefooted that morning. Sure would have been a lot smarter to have gotten the inside of the boots soaking wet.

Just about the time when I managed to make a beautiful throw around her neck, a sharp pain in the bottom of my left foot demanded my immediate attention. Limping sheepishly out to the water's edge, I handed the end of the rope to the farmer while I sat down for a look at my foot. No doubt about it, I needed stitches.

That kind old farmer insisted that I stop what I was doing and go back into town for medical attention. He promised to have the cow in a more accessible place when

I returned. So, I jumped into the cab of my truck and sped back into Hartselle.

I remembered seeing a medical clinic downtown near the post office, so I pulled up as close to the front door as I could. After a short wait, I was lead back to the exam room of the first available doctor. I had no way of knowing what a lucky day this was.

Dr. Will Crouch had been in practice in Hartselle a couple of years, and we swapped stories while he took care of the minor surgery. He became our family doctor that day and remained our trusted physician until he retired 42 years later.

Returning to my truck, I whisked through light traffic back to the farm. I know the traffic was light because it always is in Hartselle except for the night of the Christmas parade.

True to his promise, my understanding client had the cow restrained so I could get to her and deliver her beautiful, Hereford calf.

Baby, come back!

Yes, there is a famous song with those words in the title. It was written by Peter Beckett and J.C. Crowley and released in 1978. The following incident occurred 3 or 4 years before then.

Vicky (Sharrott) had just finished bathing a small black poodle, and we were sitting in the front room. Remember, at the time our office was a three-room deal. The reception was in the front, boarding, grooming and hospitalizations in the back, and everything else in the middle.

Since the wet dog was in a drying cage, Vicky made frequent trips to the back room to make sure the pet did not get overheated. Suddenly, she burst through screaming, "Baby's gone!"

She pushed through the front door without slowing down with me a step or two behind her. My first concern caused me to gaze in fear into the busy stretch of Main Street that was only a few feet from the front door.

I had already begun to imagine how dreadful the phone call to the owner was going to be. How would I ever explain this when we had no idea how the escape happened in the first place?

Instinctively, we both repeated over and over again as loudly as possible, "Baby, come back!" Our office was one of five in the same building with various other businesses renting space from the owner, Mr. Bill Gardner. All we could do was make trips around the whole building, slinging gravel and drawing attention as we rounded the corners.

On the second or third trip, Vicky darted back into the open front door and slammed it shut. Imagine my relief when I peered through the window and saw Vicky tightly holding "Baby" in her lap. During our frantic sprints, "Baby" had calmly gone inside and jumped up onto the couch intended for clientele.

I don't think we were able to see the humor in what happened until a couple of hours passed and our fearful nerves settled down.

But we've laughed countless times since then, imagining what passers-by must have thought when they witnessed the two of us racing by crying out, "Baby, come back!"

The human nail trim

If nothing else, veterinary medicine is as entertaining as plays on Broadway in New York City. You get everything from sidesplitting comedy to complicated mysteries to heart-wrenching drama. The difference is, you never know what's showing on any given day.

Right in the middle of one of those rare days when the flow of work was brisk, no pets were facing life or death afflictions, and even the weather was pleasant, an epic scene was about to unfold with no warning at all.

In our permanent building on Highway 31, two primary exam rooms lined up side by side across the hall from the reception area. The arrangement has proven for many years to be quite efficient. But, it's also easy to hear what's happening from one room to the other any time there's a pause in the action.

My business partner, Dr. Phil Gault, is blessed with an indomitable sense of humor. That's why the following event was tailor-made for him. To this day, anytime we're together, reminiscing about our years together, he'll always bring it up in the conversation, and laugh as hard as if it just happened. I love that about him, by the way.

So, I digress to the story. The skinny of the story is quite simple. An elderly, unshaven, somewhat ragged looking man walks into my exam room without a pet. That was not unusual before the Internet and what veterinarians now affectionately refer to as "Dr. Google". People who owned animals made visits to our hospital seeking our advice about all sorts of medical subjects. I now know that everyone in the office except me knew what this man was about to request of me.

In my most sincere and naïve voice, I greeted him and asked him what I could do for him. Without flinching, and with complete sincerity, his words hung in the air; "Doc, I need you to trim my nails." One look at his unwashed hands, the impressively long fingernails, and his unfeigned expression removed all doubt that he was serious.

Please understand, we never laughed at the poor man who was apparently suffering from some misunderstanding. The fun was and is kindled by my reaction. Rather than even a muted smile, I must have had that look I get when I'm silently going through options for how to respond. Yes, one of my thoughts was to honor his request and trim his nails.

If fingernail clippers were in my pocket that day, who knows what I might have done. But, I didn't have any, and that's what I explained to the fellow on the opposite side of my exam table.

As far as I know, that man could have been Howard Hughes. But, I am sure we never saw him again after our receptionist gave him directions to a local nail spa.

Laura's first farm call

Spring of 1974 brought lots of work and promise for the future of PAH which was about to celebrate a one-year anniversary. Another harbinger of good things was the presence of our first-born. Laura brought us unspeakable joy while we tried to learn the art of parenting.

The timing of her birth and the ensuing deep affection for her intensified my motivation to build a thriving practice. Even now as I'm writing, her skills as a writer and communicator have evolved into a new and undeniable motivation to try to catch up with her.

Unlike today, in 1974 and many years afterward, practicing veterinary medicine was a 24/7 kind of profession. There were no emergency animal hospitals and the number of vets treating both farm animals and pets was small. As a result, none of the 24 hours in any day was off-limits for a call to action.

One cold, cloudy, and windy Saturday afternoon I was enjoying time with four-month-old Laura in our home on Walker Road. Like every other Saturday, our office hours included 8 AM until noon. Hartselle was rural enough that Saturday was a hectic day for businesses. It was still the one day of the week when farmers came to town, and most everyone else found some free time from their Monday through Friday schedule.

For our family, Saturday afternoon was the best time for Connie to go to the grocery store. That's where she was when the pastel phone on the wall with the long curly cord rang out. As I walked over to answer it, I thought to myself, "Whatever it is will have to wait because I can't go anywhere until Connie gets back home."

"Hello," I chirped. The reply from the other end was a typically short and factual statement of the reason for the call. "Hello, this is Forrest Anders out at Massey. I've got a heifer in labor, and we need you to come help her deliver her calf." I immediately went into my explanation of the situation I was in and just how young my little daughter was at the time.

After a long silence followed by some low whispering, the sweet voice of his elderly wife came through the earpiece.

"Doctor Pearson, why don't you come on and bring that baby with you? I raised nine children, so I surely know what I'm doing. Why, one of my daughters, Doris Jernigan, goes to church with you. I keep the house nice and warm, and it'll be a treat for me to watch after that little one of yours while you're in the barn."

By the time she finished her plea, I was putty in her hands. Besides, I've always liked adventures! So, I quickly wrote a note for Connie, changed clothes, and headed out the door with my wrapped up bundle of joy. Looking back, the most significant threat to Laura's safety was the lack of a car seat or seat belt. That was true every time we traveled before those luxuries were available.

If you know Laura, you know how easygoing she is. I'm sure she never whimpered at all on the entire round trip in that old Chevy truck. And, certainly, Mrs. Anders' home was perfectly suited to keep Laura and me both at ease. However, it did take me a few minutes to calm Connie down from her hour or so of anxious waiting between reading my note and our arrival.

It's fun to remember an adventure like that one. Plus, it became a story about the new vet in town. Folks in the community were talking about Dr. Pearson's willingness to find ways to help clients and their animals.

Let me use the bathroom first!

North Alabama has a well-deserved reputation for being a "tornado alley." We were all reminded of that in

the late afternoon and evening hours of April 3, 1974.
Eight confirmed tornadoes, including four extremely
intense and long-lived storms, brought death and
destruction to Alabama. Eighty-six people died, 949 were
injured, and damages exceeded $50 million. The twisters
ravaged sixteen counties in the northern part of the state.
Many more tornadoes have come our way since then, too.

To our credit, we had a written and rehearsed plan of
action to protect our patients and ourselves whenever we
had a tornado warning in our area.

The people you work with in a small, independent
veterinary practice become far more than employees. They
become family. That family atmosphere comes through in
surprising ways at times.

As is often the case, we'd all heard the predictions of
a severe weather event for the afternoon hours. Sure
enough, mid-afternoon brought the sound of sirens and
repeated radio warnings of an impending tornado moving
roughly in our direction.

Honestly, we hear that so often I fear we take the
threat less seriously than we should. And on this particular
day, we did wait until the last possible minute to swing into
action and follow our plan to take cover in the safest place
available.

For us, that "safe place" was in the small half-bath
located in the center of the building away from any outside
doors or windows. Finally, I gave the orders for the four
of us-me and three ladies-to cram ourselves into the
bathroom.

Just as I swung the door open and motioned the
others inside, Becca King uttered her memorable words,

"Y'all wait a minute. I've got to use it first." By the time she finished and opened the door, we all sensed that the threat was over, and we might as well get back to work.

There was nothing left to do except laugh at the thought of what might have been had a tornado struck the building during those few minutes of separation.

There's a cat inside the walls.

Boarding and hospitalizing pets in a veterinary practice is a mixed bag of benefits, enormous responsibility, rewards, and headaches. I can't count the number of hours on weekends and holidays I spent cleaning runs and cages, walking and feeding pets, and administering medications to uncooperative patients. I do owe a debt of gratitude to all those who helped me do that through the years, too.

One of our most faithful clients had a risky tendency. Many people who love animals share this inclination with her. That is, they have a soft spot, which leads them to adopt pets of questionable or unknown heritage and background. When Mrs. James brought just such a cat to us in a tightly locked crate, she warned us about the female feline's streak of wildness.

Taking full responsibility for the care of her new acquisition, she brought her to us to get her spayed as soon as possible. We were to examine her and give her all the vaccinations we thought she needed. We agreed that the surgery might help to calm her down so she could become someone's permanent pet.

We decided the best course of action was to place the crate into a spacious cage complete with food and water and a soft towel, leaving the door to the box open. We thought we'd find our patient contentedly lying on that towel in the morning. Yeah, right.

Morning brought everything but contentment. As I was getting my exam room ready for the day, Debbie suddenly burst through the door holding her wounded right hand. A closer look confirmed she'd suffered significant bites and scratches. When she'd opened the cage, a vicious attack ensued, and the cat escaped her grasp.

The metal walls in the kennel area are 10 feet tall. That was no match for an adrenaline-powered mad feline. Somehow that cat clawed her way up the 6-foot rack of cages, jumped and scratched her way to the top and disappeared down into the space between the interior and exterior walls.

Of course, the implications were numerous. First, we sent Debbie to her local doctor who cleansed her wounds, made sure her tetanus prevention was up-to-date, and put her on an antibiotic. In the meantime, we called Mrs. James who was, as always, understanding and supportive. Then, the perplexing search for the missing feline began. The possible locations seemed to far outnumber the options for recovering the animal. So, we waited in the hope that she'd get hungry and return to her crate. In fact, she did return, eat her food, use the litter box, then disappear before dawn back to her hiding place.

After four days of this "cat and mouse" game, I became more and more anxious. Would Debbie need to undergo rabies prophylaxis since we had no reason to believe the cat had ever received a vaccination? Before getting advice from the local health department, I came up with another idea. We borrowed a wire trapdoor trap from animal control, placed it in a run, and loaded it with the tastiest wet cat food we could find. Then I prayed earnestly for that cat to be sitting in the trap the next morning.

I knew from experience that God answers prayer. And I had a high degree of faith my prayers for a resolution to this issue would be coming when I arrived at the hospital. It was at least an hour before anyone else would be coming in, and I said another prayer as I slowly opened the door. The sight of that cat sitting trapped and safe in that run set off some of my most heartfelt praises to God before or since.

Later in the day, we gave an injectable sedative through the wires of the trap, did our examination, performed the surgery, and gave vaccinations including one for rabies. As a precaution, we quarantined the patient for another week. That was beyond the standard limit of ten days after a biting incident.

There is no way to anticipate all the possible challenges when dealing with animals. A surprise is always waiting to happen during any day, so you learn from issues as you go along and make changes to prevent making mistakes in the future.

As a result of the "cat in the wall" episode, all untamed felines would have to remain in a crate inside a cage until two employees were available to work together. They would carefully extract the patient for immediate sedation and treatment.

Eleven cats: 78 days

The man's name was Benjamin Spivey (not his real name but a fictitious one). Even though I corresponded with him frequently for over two months, I still do not understand him or what motivated his actions. Hopefully, I did learn some valuable lessons through my encounter with him.

The summer months were consistently the busiest for us, as they are for vet practices, in general. Schools were out, so people divided their time between vacations and outdoor activities at home. The result was: 1) sharp increase in appointments for vaccinations, 2) more cases of pet injuries associated with outdoor activities, and 3) a jump in boarding business.

Mr. Spivey's arrival could not have come at a more troublesome time, which was the middle of June.

He quietly parked his van along the far edge of the parking lot, then made his way into the front door. After a brief conversation with him, Brenda let me know I needed to hear his unusual request. I think we all sensed something odd in his demeanor, but he'd learned the art of persuasion well somewhere in his past.

His story was that while on his way to Cullman, he'd become ill and needed to return to his home in Florence until the next morning. He asked us to board his cats overnight so he could get home, get some rest without having to care for the cats, then return the next day to go on to Cullman. As I look back, it's easy to see we should have "smelled a rat" and turned him down. Especially when he revealed that there were 11 cats we'd need to board "just one night, of course."

My explanation that we didn't have 11 cages available, meaning the cats would have to share four spaces didn't bother him at all. Since about half of them were kittens, that arrangement would work just fine.

We made a file for our new client and assured him we'd only charge for four spaces instead of 11. He assured us he'd be happy to pay the amount tomorrow when he picked up his pets.

While standing behind the counter watching his van pull out onto the highway, a wave of suspicion rolled over me. Something told me not to hold my breath until I saw that aging vehicle drive back into our parking lot.

As you can easily guess, our phone calls to Mr. Spivey went unanswered during the following week. We decided to send a letter urging him to get his cats and pay the invoice which we included in the envelope. Miraculously, a few days late an envelope showed up in our mailbox with a check for about a third of his debt and a promise to wrap things up soon.

That process of sending letters and invoices continued for weeks. The payment amount dwindled with each check we received. In the meantime, those kittens were becoming grown cats, which meant more expenses for food, litter, and labor.

Late one afternoon Vicky called out to me from the kennel, yelling, "Doc, you gotta see this!" Vicky was standing a few feet back from the kennels so all the cats could see her wave a can of food back and forth. Every last feline's head and shoulders swayed back and forth in perfect unison with their eyes fixed on her hand. When she stopped, they stopped. When she moved her hand again, the hilarious dancing cat show cranked up again.

Finally, after seven unchanging weeks of hoping for the best, I called a local lawyer for advice. I wanted assurance that it would be within our rights to take this herd of cats to the local animal shelter.

I called this particular lawyer because we went to church together, he was an elderly gentleman with years of experience, and Hartselle had already named a street in his honor. The response I got from him seemed to reflect his age more than any of the other reasons for my choosing to call him. He said, "Why doc, just go ahead and put 'em all to sleep and be done with it!"

I wasn't about to take that advice. But it did give me some freedom to figure out a less drastic option. I remember smiling when the solution came to me.

I called my friend and bank president, Dennis, and said we need to go fishing. We'd fished together a lot, so he had no reason to suspect anything out of the ordinary. Conveniently, one of our favorite destinations was Pickwick Lake near Florence Alabama.

Dennis did have some questions when we met in the PAH parking lot, and I started loading five cardboard pet carriers into the back seat of my Chevy pickup with the boat attached and ready to go fishing. After my explanation, he got a huge laugh out of my predicament and was soon all in for this little adventure.

Driving right past the boat launch without stopping was hard. But we were on a mission to find the home of Benjamin Spivey in downtown Florence before wetting a hook.

It turned out to be one of those old, two-story homes in the original section of town - one of those that people often invest in to remodel. Like most of those, there was a large wooden front porch with well-worn rocking chairs and a ragged swing.

When I mashed hard on the doorbell, we could hear it chiming loudly inside the house. The old familiar van was right there in the driveway, so I pulled open the screen door and banged on the glass of the front door. No response came from inside the house.

By this time I was just done. Done with trying to do the right thing. Done with being patient with Benjamin Spivey. Done with delaying a much-needed fishing trip on the Tennessee River.

Dennis and I carefully placed the five carriers near the front door and double-checked each one to make sure none had jarred open during the trip. After knocking one last time I reached into my shirt pocket and pulled out a note and invoice, which I wedged securely between the door and wall. As we left, I vowed to learn from this experience and stop acting so naïve, pay attention to my gut feelings, and become more assertive.

Our fishing trip went well, and I arrived home after dark. Connie stuck her head out the back door and said, "You know that guy from Florence you've been talking about so much? He called me this afternoon and said tell you to expect to hear from his lawyer soon for abandoning his cats." Honestly, I didn't care. I just thought, "Well bring it on, big guy!" Besides, if he ever paid me for boarding his 11 cats for 78 days, I'd have enough money to pay for a good lawyer if I needed one.

A most memorable horse call.

For several years while I was still practicing solo we closed the office at noon on Wednesdays. Many of those days my Dad would come to Hartselle at closing time with his boat in tow so we could head to Smith Lake for an afternoon of fishing.

On one of those Wednesday mornings, I got a call at about 10:45 AM to go to the Neel community and exam a lame horse. The directions were to turn right at the Neel intersection and stop at the second house on the right.

Nothing was happening at the office at the time, so I jumped into the truck and sped out Highway 36 West on my way to see the horse and try to get back before noon. So, I pulled into the driveway of the second house on the right, walked up on the porch and after knocking on the door was greeted by a man and his wife. They cordially invited me to come in and have a seat. Trying to be sociable I sat down on the sofa in their living room.

After a few minutes of casual conversation, I decided to say as nicely as I could, "Well, I guess we better go see about your horse." They looked at each other and laughed a little in a way that expressed a feeling of great relief and said, "Uh, we don't own a horse."

I always wore a necktie because that's what we were taught to do in vet school. The tie, coupled with my tan coveralls had convinced that couple that I was the game warden. Most of the time that would not have been a big deal, of course. But it just so happened that earlier in the day they had gotten a little carried away and killed way over the legal limit of squirrels. So they were scared to death that the game warden had caught up with them and was about to arrest them.

After a good laugh, I went on to the house next door and finally found my equine patient whose owner was beginning to wonder what happened to the vet.

One of many humbling experiences.

While in our office on Main Street I got a call from Mr. Harvey Yates. Mr. Yates owned a sheet metal business just around the corner, and he had a small farm out East of Hartselle. He asked me to go with him out to the farm to treat a young calf for the scours (diarrhea).

That poor little fellow was weak and dehydrated, and I knew saving him was a long shot. But, of course, I had to give it my best effort. So, I did treat him with injections, oral sulfadiazine, and even infused a liter of fluid intravenously. After leaving Mr. Yates with some meds and oral fluid replacements, I felt reasonably good about a positive outcome. But not wanting to over-promise, I still indicated this would be touch and go for a couple more days.

A few days later when I saw Mr. Yates in town, I asked him about his sick calf. When Mr. Yates tried to talk fast, he had a pretty severe stuttering issue. So, he looked at me and said something like, "Doc, he ga, ga, got fi, fi, fine after I, I, I ga, ga, gave him a pi, pi, pint of whiskey!"

8 HALL OF FAME EMPLOYEES

Every good and perfect gift is from above, coming down from the Father of the heavenly lights, who does not change like shifting shadows. James 1:17

From "Preface" to "Conclusion," this will be the most challenging chapter for me to write. Not because I can't think of anything to say. No, it's difficult because I know my words will never be able to capture the depth and richness of our experiences together or the extent of my gratitude to each one for their loyalty and continuing friendship.

I chose the Bible verse for this chapter for a particular reason. PAH grew from the humblest beginning. We opened our doors as a 100% family business. I was the doctor, the CEO, the COO, the CMO, the CFO, the groomer, the janitor, and the nurse. Connie, the musician, was our pregnant receptionist during the first couple of months.

As we grew, extraordinary people showed up for work. I never put an ad in the paper, contacted the employment office, or even put a "Help Wanted" sign in the window. Considering all I know now, and how well things worked out, there's no doubt that each of the following people was the result of divine intervention.

Connie Pearson

We got married on March 20, 1971, and I began my senior year of vet school just over a week later. Although madly in love, I had no way of knowing how lucky that day was for me. She's always been the spark I've needed to get me moving forward.

Officially, day one of PAH was April 2, 1973. When we got to the tiny office on Main Street that morning, we found ourselves surrounded by furniture we'd bought at garage sales. There was an old brown sofa for clients, a small 4-legged table with one drawer, and a straight back chair behind it. We'd painted the table and chair an olive green.

A standard black, rotary dial telephone sat one corner of the table, and a small metal recipe file box sat in the other corner. No, we didn't need recipes. That box held index cards, which we'd soon need for new client records. Pulling out the drawer gave access to what we affectionately called "the money box." It was a simple gray metal box with no dividers and a lock that hadn't worked in a while.

People are attracted to Connie. Everyone who carries on a conversation with her wants to be her friend. In the beginning, getting calls to farms was much easier than getting pet owners into the office. The people with pets who gradually trickled in were almost always women.

When those ladies met Connie and connected with her, they concluded her husband must be a good man, too. A foundation of loyal clients was born.

That pattern repeated itself through the years, even though Connie worked in the office for only a few months. She became well known and respected as our church pianist, as a competent piano teacher for scores of children, and then as the music teacher in the school system. Through all those years, lots of clients were prone to accept me because of her reputation.

The environment of a veterinary hospital is not compatible with a pregnant person suffering from morning sickness. The last straw came in the form of an unsuspecting salesman who thrust his air freshener product under Connie's nose. I don't know who left the room faster, Connie as she dashed for the bathroom or the salesman getting back into his car. Regardless, we knew it was time to hire our first employee as her replacement.

Kathy Jenkins

About the time Connie reached her limit in veterinary practice, a conversation was taking place in a home not far from town. I'd treated some cattle for Mr. "Dude" Kelley, and he must have gotten a good impression. He encouraged his daughter, Kathy, to go and see if that new vet needed any help. She took his advice without delay, and the timing could not have been better.

Kathy was the right person at the right time. She had experience with animals from growing up on a farm. She had an excellent voice for answering the phone and interacting with clients. She and her family were well-known and respected around Hartselle. She saw this job as something she very much wanted to do, and she brought a solid work ethic.

I don't know what Kathy expected her job to be, but she would soon realize no job title could convey the array of duties she'd be involved in every day. Of course, it all began with answering the phone. Regardless of when it might ring, I needed her help with holding pets for exams, assisting with surgeries, bathing pets, discharging patients, and keeping the place clean.

Her first disappointment came as I dashed out the back door to a farm call. As my hand grabbed the handle on the door of my pickup, I noticed she was right behind me. "Did I forget something?" "No. I don't think so," she said as she hurried around to the far side of the truck. "Uh, sorry Kathy, but we need you to stay here and answer the phone while I'm gone." Being a typical clueless male, I failed to realize she thought the job included farm calls. A few months later when Vicky joined our staff, they convinced me to let them alternate going with me to farms.

Kathy proved her worth many times over the ten years she worked at PAH. A daunting challenge lumbered in one summer afternoon in the form of a massive Bassett Hound named, "Tuff-luck." The poor guy had a long history of recurring constipation. When he came to us, he was completely stopped up and painfully arching his back and straining every few steps. Vets have to be creative. In this case, we unhooked the door off a cage and balanced it across the edges of our claw-foot bathtub, another garage sale purchase that's still in use today.

After sedating Tuff-luck, we laid his massive body on the makeshift rack over the tub and started the unpleasant task of dislodging the rock-hard feces. Using a combination of soapy enemas and careful gouging with

gloved fingers, I finally removed enough to give him a
chance to finish the job overnight. As it turned out, that
procedure had to be repeated three consecutive days to get
him cleaned out. Kathy stayed right there, keeping the tub
rinsed out and the patient steady without complaining. No,
trust me, you cannot imagine the aroma permeating that
little room the whole time.

One of the large animal calls Kathy made with me
was to Mr. John Knight's farm for seasonal herd work. We
needed Kathy to record everything we did to each animal
as they came through the chute. Besides records for the
Knight Polled Hereford Farm, there were stacks of
government ledgers for documents about testing cattle for
TB and Brucellosis plus more records for any heifers
receiving a brucellosis vaccination.

A day was set aside every March for working the
Knight farm. The weather in Alabama is quite
unpredictable that time of year. But springtime consistently
seems to have an invigorating effect on animals and
humans alike. Every bovine coming through the chute
displayed evidence of increased strength and decreased
patience. That translates into lots of noise, lots of mud,
feces, urine, and saliva flying in all directions from the
antics of each patient as they fought against confinement
in a very narrow space with their necks squeezed by cold
metal bars.

Kathy set up a table and chair a safe distance from
the chute, but close enough for clear communication while
we worked through the herd. That worked great until a
huge bull escaped and headed straight for the table. Kathy
looked up when she heard us screaming, "Run!" Between
the beast, the March wind, and Kathy's quick exit, the
papers got scattered far and wide across the wet mud, grass
and wild onions around the barn. Thankfully, nobody got

injured. All the documents stayed close enough for full recovery, and the bull got cajoled back to where he belonged without much delay.

Vicky Sharrott

"Oh me, I can't see a patient right now." The words blurted out anxiously when I saw a smiling young lady making her way from the parking lot toward the front door. We were still on Main Street then, so we're only talking about two or three steps. I was dashing through the clinic toward the back door and my truck to drive to a dairy farmer and his milk cow suffering from what's called "milk fever." It was a typical condition back then. It happens as a result of dangerously low levels of calcium in the blood, which is related to the massive amounts of milk produced in the first weeks after calving. The treatment of infusing a calcium solution into the vein is not complicated, but it is an emergency and requires close attention to the heart rate as the bloodstream takes on the calcium.

When I heard the words, "I've come to apply for a job," I was relieved for three reasons. First, it meant no delay in getting to the farm. Equally important was that I had realized we'd grown to the point of needing more help. Most importantly, I sensed something about this person that made me trust her. I simply said, "Great, be here at eight o'clock in the morning." That was the beginning of a twenty-year relationship between PAH and Vicky Sharrott. It also marked the start of a friendship between her family and ours that is healthy and meaningful to this day. Our kids say they can't remember a time when there wasn't a Vicky Sharrott in their lives.

There were a few years when Kathy and Vicky worked together, so lots of my favorite stories involved both of them. I do know that one of the first things Kathy told Vicky was, "I've never seen anybody make such messes to clean up." Apparently, I was not so good about keeping things neat around the office.

The very first day Vicky worked at PAH a client brought a pregnant Chihuahua in for help delivering her puppies. The problem was evident. The fetus' head was too large and was trapped just short of making it through. I had Vicky hold her while I injected a local anesthetic, performed an episiotomy, and delivered the puppy.

By the time another puppy was delivered, and the suturing finished, it was clear that Vicky loved being involved in the procedure and she loved learning new things. I don't believe she ever lost her enthusiasm throughout her twenty years as a veterinary assistant.

For whatever reason, Vicky had confidence in me from the beginning. I needed that because I was about as insecure as I could be. So, I worked hard to seem at least confident enough to keep from disappointing her. Her encouragement helped me to practice at a higher level as I began to believe in myself more and more.

I don't know how many fractured canine limbs Vicky and I repaired surgically, but it seems like there were hundreds. On many occasions, when it seemed impossible to manipulate bone fragments into alignment, Vicky would say, "Come on Doc. Get mad, and you'll get 'em together." It worked every time.

Orthopedic surgery is not only physically stressful, it can be downright dangerous, too. We used an electric drill to drive steel pins through bones to hold fractured pieces in place for healing. During one of those procedures, Vicky operated the drill while I held the fragments in place. Suddenly and without warning, the pin went too far, exited the bone and dug into my finger. I told her not to worry, just back it out so we could try again. She did, I donned a fresh pair of gloves, and the pet, the doctor, and Vicky did just fine without any complications.

Vicky was always extremely loyal to PAH, and she fiercely protected it when needed. For example, now and then someone would come into the hospital and Vicky would whisper, "Doc, he still owes you money." (She could always quote the correct amount, too.) And, she didn't hesitate to discreetly mention it to the delinquent patron before services were rendered. She can tell you to this day the names of several who never paid their debt to PAH.

Vicky helped raise our kids, too. She took it all in stride when one or more of them had to be left at the hospital while Connie hauled another one to the doctor in Decatur.

Lynn Thrasher

We all need a person in our lives who has a calming effect, someone with a personality bent toward tranquility. Lynn filled that need for me when I desperately needed it. Dr. Steve Pearson looked good on the outside, I guess, but internally I was a bundle of frayed nerves. I fretted when we weren't swamped with work, and I worried whether I was up to the task when it came along in bunches. Anxiety skyrocketed when a call involved an equine patient.

Lynn was comfortable around horses because of his experience with them. And, some of his friends owned a horse farm near Hartselle. Robert Drinkard came by the office to let Lynn and me know about a mare with a retained placenta. The mass of tissue also called the "afterbirth" should exit as the foal is born. Remaining inside the uterus, it will cause severe infection leading to death in a short period. On the drive to the farm, my mind was racing and digging through everything I'd learned about how to manage a case like this one. Lynn's question, "What do 'ya think, Doc?" conveyed a quiet confidence free of any hint of doubt that I might be unsure of myself.

As my left hand probed through a vaginal exam, my fear was confirmed. The placenta's attachment to the uterine wall was too tight for manual removal.
Forcing it loose would likely cause devastating tears inside the uterus. So, I decided to inject oxytocin and pray it worked its magic. We were all elated when after a few agonizing minutes, the hormone did its job of squeezing the uterine muscles and the fleshy, glistening placenta fell to the ground with a splash.

Jennifer Garner

Jennifer worked at PAH for quite a while as a volunteer. Her persistence and the skills she learned eventually developed her into a valuable addition to our staff.

She was there when we installed our first computer for the practice. Within a few days, we were all convinced it was the worst decision possible. None of us had any experience with computers, so the thing efficiently ate up huge chunks of time instead of saving any. Efficiency was why we got it in the first place! Now I realize what a simple program it was, but it seemed like a hopeless maze for several agonizing weeks.

Like all vet practices, a high percentage of our surgical cases involved procedures of sterilizing pets. Clients often get confused by the terminology describing those operations, so let's set the record straight. Female dogs and cats get spayed, while male dogs and cats get neutered.

Clients have been known to present a female dog and announce things like, "Doc, I want you to take her Honda out." Or, "He's here to get neutralized." One morning a client arrived on his way to work, dropping off two cats to be spayed. Before leaving, he said, "By the way, I want you to leave her ovaries in." When I asked him the obvious question, "Why in the world would you expect me to do that?" he quickly answered, "Because I read on the internet that it's better for them to keep their ovaries." As soon as I explained such a decision would ensure the cats would maintain regular periods of estrus for the rest of their lives, he signed the release form for the standard procedure.

The least complex of those procedures is the neutering of tomcats. We routinely performed those under anesthesia with a combination injection of ketamine and acepromazine. The advantage is that you inject it into the muscle, the patient becomes unconscious quickly, and there is pain control during the procedure. The disadvantage is the slow recovery period, which was usually 60 to 90 minutes.

Jennifer assisted me with a cat neuter around 2:30 one afternoon. As soon as I finished, I went on to an exam room to see patients while she cleaned up and kept an eye on the patient, which would remain motionless on the table for a half-hour or so. Apparently, she was reaching up to place some instruments on the top shelf about the time one of our highly efficient part-time high school students came into work.

We'd trained him to go ahead and get busy as soon as he arrived after school. Naturally, the "dead cat" on the table caught his attention before he noticed anything else.

Thinking the patient came in for euthanasia, he gently placed it into a plastic bag and headed for the freezer. Thank the Lord for Jennifer who anxiously inquired, "What's in that bag?" Words cannot convey the level of angst and sorrow she saved us all by interrupting that patient's untimely trip to the deep freeze.

You can't know Jennifer without liking her. She's easy going and pleasant and never involved in any drama as some people are prone to be. All of us associated with her through working at PAH are fortunate to have her as a friend.

My relationship with Jennifer was severely tested by an incident one afternoon while I was out on a farm call. This spring day was one of those that started out cold in the morning and then became hot and sunny by the afternoon. The outside wall of my exam room had a large sliding window above a narrow ledge, which we built in at about chin level. We kept displays and a few small cartons of heartworm preventives up there for convenience and to add interest to the room. In fact, there was a glass jar there with a preserved heart from a dog who'd passed away from a heavy burden of 10- to 12-inch-long heartworms.

When I came back that afternoon, Jennifer met me in the hallway with a severely sad expression and tears in her eyes. She had innocently slid the window above the ledge open, just as we'd all done many times to let in a little fresh air. The jar of heartworms sticking out of the pickled heart and the other displays were still where they belonged. But, a puff of wind came through the opened window strong enough to move the blinds and knock the antique Red Goose onto the floor where it shattered, irreparably. Not only was it an antique, but it also came from my grandparents' clothing store in Moulton where they sold Red Goose shoes for many years.

Yes, losing that piece of personal history hurt a lot. But, it truly was an accident just waiting to happen from the day I put that old goose up there in the window myself. In the end, it was my fault for not leaving such a treasure locked up in a closet at home. I realized all that right away and assured Jennifer she shouldn't worry about it.

And yes, I treasure Jennifer's friendship far more than any sentimental object.

Brenda Hall

For far too long we raced around answering the phone, checking patients in and out, and trying to greet clients in the midst of all the medical responsibilities we had. Kathy, Vicky, and Connie finally convinced me it was time for a full-time receptionist.

The solution to our problem came along just in the nick of time. Brenda was efficient, great at answering the phone, greeting clients, and most of all, keeping everything clerical in order. We could not have asked for more.

Clients loved Brenda. In all the years she worked at PAH, we never heard any complaints from customers. That's quite an accomplishment when you consider so many clients are anxious, nervous, and worried when they bring a sick or injured pet to a veterinary hospital.

Brenda contributed plenty of insightful suggestions for improving patient care. She requested earphones several times. They would free up her hands to pull records and write notes while talking on the phone. I regret that we never granted her request. Now I wish I'd listened to Brenda and installed earphones to our system.

Becca King

In the South, we often describe people like Becca as, "Quite a character." Like so many of our phrases, you have to know a little about the person to get the intended portrayal. But it does describe a person who's blessed with some unusual characteristics. In Becca's case, they are all excellent qualities.

Her sense of humor is never out of the picture. She can make people laugh along with her in almost any circumstance. Sometimes, if things get a little dull, she'll manufacture some humor.

After seeing several patients on a busy day, I realized I kept hearing Becca and her fellow pet nurse Liz laughing back in the exam room while I was out in the lobby giving clients some last minute instructions. Of course, as soon as I could get free, I asked, "What in the world is so funny?" They looked at each other and knew there was no way to escape telling the truth. They had devised a game. Before each client entered the room for an exam, they came up with a word. The challenge was to see who could get the pet owner to say the word first. You can imagine them keeping a straight face until the client was safely out of hearing. The fun soon wore off, and this happened only a few times, I'm sure.

Another one of their favorites involved assisting me with anal gland expressions while the client was present. In case you aren't familiar with it, dogs have a pair of sacs underneath the skin on either side of the anus. The pouches contain a stinky liquid, which sometimes fails to empty properly. When that happens, the dog will be seen scooting along the ground (or carpet) and licking himself a lot. That's when clients show up to have the sacs emptied.

The procedure requires plastic exam gloves and some cotton to catch the liquid when it comes flying out, potentially soiling every article of clothing in the room. When done correctly, a ball of cotton about the size of the palm of your hand is all you need. On several occasions, Liz or Becca would give me a cotton ball the size of my head. Everybody in the room got a belly laugh out of that.

Becca was there when I "retired." I put that word in quotations because instead of "retiring," I just happened to switch to a new career. Connie and I sold the practice and served four years as missionaries in Ecuador. As I left on my final day at PAH, Becca playfully tried to hold back the truck as I drove out of the parking lot.

When we came home, I acquired a position at Banfield which is a corporate vet practice located in PetSmart. Becca came and worked there with me for almost six years.

Carrie Wallace

In February 1999, Carrie joined our team from a teller position at the local bank. That experience helped make her the outstanding receptionist we needed to assist Brenda with growing responsibilities in the front office.

Before long, she'd figured out ways to make herself even more valuable by getting Becca to cross train her in vet assistant duties.

During some of that training, she got a little confused somehow while running a blood chemistry panel on one of our patients. Our blood analyzer would give us values on a dozen blood chemistries results on the spot. Since testing only took a few minutes, we used it numerous times every day.

It was reported to me just recently, several years later, that Carrie managed to run 12 creatinine disks on a single patient!

Anyone who's worked with the public in a veterinary practice knows that some people tend to make you a little nervous. Carrie experienced that when a former school teacher named Carol brought her pet cat named Frizzy in for an exam and vaccines. Everything was going fine with the check-in and inquiries about Frizzy's health status. When I was ready to see the patient, Carrie announced loud and clear to a full waiting room, "You can bring Carol on back now."

Carrie is one of those people who can take it all in stride and learn from mistakes. In fact, after 19 years, she's the only "Hall of Famer" still working at PAH.

9 STUDENTS WHO BECAME VETS OR VET TECHS

Few things were more fulfilling to me than hiring young kids who aspired to become veterinarians. It was always a priority for me, probably because I never had that opportunity myself. There were two reasons I missed the chance to work in a veterinary practice during high school. First, I didn't decide to become a veterinarian until my senior year. The other reason is that I needed to work forty or more hour weeks at as high a salary as possible to help pay my way through Auburn.

I am exceptionally proud to have played a small part in the meaningful careers of these young folks. I consider them to be my greatest contribution to our profession.

Barry Stewart

Barry may have been the first student to work at PAH. He took piano lessons from Connie.

It was evident from the beginning that he'd become

an excellent veterinary doctor. His Dad and Granddad both operated businesses in Hartselle for many years, and his family owned a cattle farm in nearby Lawrence County. As I explained earlier, it didn't work out for us to work together after he graduated from vet school, but I'll never forget the day he called to let me know he was opening his own practice about a mile south of mine. I was proud of him and glad to know there'd be a quality colleague down the street for years to come.

Dr. Stewart served our profession by his activities with the local and state associations. He served as the secretary/treasurer of the North Alabama Veterinary Medical Association for many years. Best of all, we still enjoy a healthy friendship and enjoy visiting from time to time.

David Crouch

David is another one of Connie's former piano students who worked at PAH as a high school student. His Dad, Dr. Will Crouch, was our family doctor for 42 years before he retired. I understand there was a time in the Crouch home that when someone called their phone and asked for Dr. Crouch, they'd ask, "Do you want the two-legged or four-legged one?"

After graduation, David was anxious to join Dr. Gault and me at PAH. We advised him that working at another location for a couple of years would give him some valuable experience before joining us. He did just that, came back to Hartselle and has practiced at PAH ever since.

I hope you've noticed already how convinced I am that God provided what we needed just when we needed it throughout my career. His intervention clearly guided Dr.

Gault and Dr. Crouch (the four-legged version).

I mention that specifically here because of a major life event that began to unfold around Christmas of 2001. By the end of January 2002, Connie and I were sure God had called us to serve as full-time missionaries. By then, both doctors were ready to buy me out and release me to follow God's direction. No one can appreciate how significant that is unless you understand how difficult it normally is to find buyers for a veterinary practice.

Dr. David Crouch is still practicing alongside Dr. Gault at Pearson Animal Hospital.

Todd Thomas

Todd came to us through a career program at his high school just after getting his driver's license. He ended up working at PAH some afternoons, most weekends, and at least part of almost all school breaks until the beginning of his 3rd year of vet school. We worked out a plan for him to work alongside Dr. Barry Stewart, which allowed him more exposure to large animal medicine.

I don't have any statistics, but I'm pretty sure more aspiring students decided not to pursue veterinary careers than those who eventually became veterinarians. Interestingly, Todd says that he watched me suture a large laceration on a pet dog his first day at work. Who knew he'd get his DVM at Auburn, finish a surgery residency at NC State, and attain the status of Diplomate, American College of Veterinary Surgeons? That's quite an achievement! After a twenty-year career as a US Army veterinarian, he now works for them and cares for service dogs.

He remembers a canine patient who came in seriously

injured by hay conditioner. Multiple lacerations included complete exposure of one testicle. When I recommended finishing the castration, the owner objected and requested saving the remaining one. It turned out he'd promised a friend he could breed the dog with his female. As far as we know, that dog not only survived but became a doggy daddy, too.

Surely you've picked up on the family-like friendships we all enjoyed at PAH. Todd's brother Eric worked there, too. In addition to a career in agriculture, a couple of years ago I had the privilege of attending Eric's pastoral ordination service.

Debbie (Palmer) Whitlock

None of us could have imagined the vibrant future that began to unfold on the day 13-year-old Debbie Palmer showed up to work part-time at PAH. She was more than just another young girl who dreamed of becoming a veterinarian because she loved animals. Yes, that was her dream at age thirteen. But, she was wise enough to keep her options open and discover what suited her best.

Like all students, she initially worked in the kennel doing the "dirty" jobs of cleaning cages and runs, feeding, and bathing and exercising pets. Her work ethic, politeness, and ability to work well with our team earned her the right to work "up front" with the doctors and vet assistants.

Being up front, she often watched surgeries, went on farm calls, and carefully observed me, the veterinarian, at work. Debbie says, "I loved the clinic so much that I convinced my parents to let me go to school half the day and work the other half for my senior year." By then she'd become a valuable contributor to our team.

In her own words, Debbie communicates the essence of why I hired young students with dreams of pursuing a career in veterinary medicine. "It was in that year that I watched you work. I had to decide what to do about college. I observed that you spent most of your time with the people, coaching them, informing them, comforting them, etc. But as technicians, Vicki and Jennifer got to do most of their work with the animals. I decided that the path with more animal exposure was the one for me- and applied to the Veterinary Technician School at Snead State- in Boaz, Alabama."

When she married a naval officer and found herself often moving, that Vet Tech degree made it easy for her to find work quickly. Before long, she was licensed in 5 states! Eventually, they landed in College Station, Texas, and Debbie started working as a small animal vet tech at the Texas A&M College of Veterinary Medicine. For three years she served as the lead second shift tech in ICU. That was followed by three more years assisting Dr. Theresa Fossum in general surgery at the small animal clinic. That working relationship led to a significant opportunity. The following is an explanation in her words.

"Dr. Fossum was just at the beginning phase of the first edition of her surgery book. She would bring the pages along to read and edit as we traveled the hour and a half to and from Austin. She was also on the edge of doing some really cool cardiovascular research. She had done surgery on a Yorkie that belonged to Dr. Michael DeBakey's wife. And as it turned out, he was working on a project, but not having much luck with the animal trials for the FDA. He reached out to her and before I knew it, she had hired me to be her head technician over her research. My work in that position allowed me the opportunity to fly in a Texas A&M jet to Houston to escort Dr. DeBakey back to the College of Veterinary Medicine. We were also invited down to Baylor hospital to watch him perform surgery. We worked on many projects that directly benefitted human medicine."

Brandi McDaniel

Brandi's mom and Connie worked together at Burleson Elementary School. Brandi got her mom to ask Connie if we needed any help at PAH, and her timing was perfect. Lucky for us, Brandi worked there from 1984 until 1995.

After earning degrees from Calhoun Community College and the University of North Alabama, she received a Veterinary Technology degree from Snead State. That enabled her to work eight years in the Auburn University College of Veterinary Medicine as a licensed veterinary technician. Since then, she's worked in that capacity at several high-end veterinary hospitals in North Alabama.

I loved reading the following quotes from an email Brandi sent me recently about her experiences at PAH.

"The time I spent at PAH taught me to work as a team and to help one another. I learned that everyone is valued and that no matter what part you play, it all works together for the good of PAH."

I thought nobody ever heard what I must have said a thousand times!

"I learned work could be fun and exciting and the workers can be like family. I learned how to correctly give injections, assist in surgery, bathe pets, walk dogs, do dental cleanings, trim nails, and so much more."

We both fondly remember the time "Hakuna Matata" from "The Lion King" was playing on the radio while she assisted me in surgery. When I sincerely asked her, "Why are they singing about a cool avocado?" she almost doubled over laughing.

10 RABIES CLINICS

... each of them may eat and drink, and find satisfaction in all their toil – this is the gift of God. Ecclesiastes 3:13

Ah, the beautiful month of June! The days are long, hot, and humid. All the leaves are green and lush. June is a great month for fishing on the Tennessee River. And for decades, June has been Rabies Clinic month across the state of Alabama.

The fresh, damp air of early morning belies the sultry heat that will dominate the rest of the day. More accurately, we're about to enjoy three days' work pressed into seven hours of intense community service. It's rabies clinic day!

None of us pays any attention as the three of us sway toward the passenger seat when my pickup truck careens almost on two wheels as we leave the clinic parking lot, cross the median, and head north toward the first stop of the day. Vicky and Kathy are too busy going over their mental checklist. "Plenty of syringes?" Check. "Hundreds of doses of vaccine in the cooler?" Check. "Five or six sleeves of rabies tags?" Check. "Three or four packs of rabies certificates?" Check. "Portable table and chair?" Check. "Plenty of leashes?" Check. "Poster with location and times of today's stops?" "Oh no, we'll have to go back to get that. Sorry about that, doc." This time we WILL turn through the median on two wheels. We cannot afford to be late to the first stop at 7:00 AM.

Luckily, the adrenaline released by the annual anticipation of a busy and fun day racing around rural Morgan County, Alabama, woke us all up early enough to allow for a quick backtrack and still make it on time. This day was not our first rodeo, um, rabies clinic. We were there a few years before when 800-plus dogs showed up over the course of a Monday and Tuesday morning marathon. But now, the whole clinic is compressed into one hectic Saturday morning.

Who knows how early in the morning folks begin to gather at the first stop of the day? I just know there's always a good crowd waiting, even when we arrive a few minutes early. Every head swivels in unison as they follow our truck across the parking lot for a clue as to where we'll set up. Today is not their first trip to a rabies clinic, either, so they appreciate the advantage of getting in line first.

Life in Alabama turns on wheels of tradition. Think fried catfish and hushpuppies. Never overlook fried chicken and potato salad. Oh yes, unwavering allegiance to one of two state football teams. Then there's my personal favorite: kids persistently answering adults with "Yes ma'am," or "Yes sir."

Attend one rabies clinic, and you'll realize it qualifies as a traditional institution. You'd think that many people in a small parking lot, all wanting the same thing, would create chaos and at least a few verbal confrontations. But, no, that never happened in my years of working in the middle of it all. You'd soon realize you're witnessing a social event. Farmers spend the time complaining about the weather and politics. The ladies pass the time bragging about the superiority of their pet's appearance and behavior. The younger generation sees this as a chance to visit with a classmate of the opposite gender they haven't seen since school ended in May.

On the other hand, all the excitement often proved to be a little too much for a few of the dogs. Ninety percent of the time, canines of all breeds, shapes, and sizes stood in line beside their family and behaved incredibly well. The problems usually involved one who'd been cooped up in a crate on a truck bed, hearing but unable to see the commotion occurring outside their line of view. The worst case of such fear and anxiety that I remember involved dogs confined to the floorboard of the front seat in an uncomfortably warm vehicle. The small open space in the windows was enough to prevent heat stroke while at the same time creating who knows what kind of threatening visions in a pet's mind from the limited information pouring into his sense of hearing.

I hate to admit it, but the following scenario occurred two mornings in a row back when the clinics occurred on Mondays and Tuesdays. On both occasions, the owner swung the front door open and pointed to my patient curled up on the floorboard between the seat and the glove compartment. Realizing how awkward it would be for the owner to crawl onto the front seat, hold the animal, and give me room to get a needle into the patient, my lack of patience overrode my wisdom. I hurriedly reached in to give the vaccine unassisted. You guessed it. In a flash, fangs penetrated the tender flesh between the thumb and forefinger of my left hand. The sad story is, I repeated the same mistake the very next morning and got identical wounds in my right hand.

I don't know if I was mostly gullible, naïve, or too trusting as a young doctor. I like to think it was a combination of all three, with the third option being dominant. Regardless of the reality, Vicky found a sneaky way to take advantage of it. Not wanting me to know she was enjoying a "smoke break," she'd go on and on about how she loved to roam through cemeteries and read the inscriptions. I took the bait, gave her a few minutes to "enjoy some tombstones" while we loaded up for the trip to the next stop. While I was busy, she found a suitably high marker, stooped down behind it and inhaled a few draws. I may never have figured it out, but after she quit smoking, I guess her burden of guilt compelled her to confess. I still smile about that trickery every time it comes to mind.

It's easy to overlook the important role veterinarians play in public health. Anyone who's taken a pet to the local vet for rabies vaccination has observed and participated in the public health role of veterinary medicine.

At the turn of the twentieth century, human rabies was not uncommon in rural America. I remember my grandparents' stories of the first-hand observance of neighbors dying from that horrible disease they knew as hydrophobia. Although often mispronounced as something like, "hygophobie," the name came about from one effect of the rabies virus, which left victims unable to swallow.

The history of rabies infection in dogs and cats is sad, indeed. Before canine rabies vaccination became mandatory by law, millions of "stray" dogs suffered extermination as the accepted means of controlling human rabies. Mercifully, that changed dramatically when widespread canine vaccination was instituted after WWII.

Rabies clinics started as a means to encourage vaccination of dogs kept by rural residents who rarely traveled into town. Plus, taking along a canine for a veterinary visit was a rarity. So, as a means to eliminate rabies, clinics were scheduled at churches, small community stores, or other familiar landmarks. Local veterinary associations developed the schedule, which was then advertised mainly with posters nailed to trees and utility poles around the county. Later, ads were placed in newspapers as well.

More often than not, one or two dog owners quietly stood back until the final patient neared the registration table. About that time, they'd muster their most humble expression and say, "Hey doc, we couldn't get our dogs up here this morning. Would you mind stopping by the house and vaccinate 'em there?" Even though such a deviation from the route invariably put us behind, we usually agreed to their request.

One of those pleas only involved a walk across the road from the church parking lot. However, our prospective patient, a large breed dog, which will remain undisclosed, was running full speed along the chain link fence around his large yard behind the owner's home. All of the man's coaxing, yelling, and calf roping with a leash proved futile. Finally, after an inordinate passage of valuable time, he sheepishly admitted that - barring me performing a real miracle - there was no hope of restraining his dog even for a quick injection. He finally said, "Doc, you see that small building in the middle of my yard? That's my workshop, and sometimes I cannot come out to walk to my house for fear of this dog." I advised him to consider some alternatives, which included coming by the office to pick up some tranquilizer tablets to feed the dog, then calling me to go back for another attempt at vaccinating his pet. I never heard from him again.

As I mentioned, state law mandated rabies vaccination of all dogs, and in later years, cats. For the sake of facilitating compliance, veterinary teams conducted annual clinics across rural areas. The service took place near the front doors of owners of dogs and cats. Not only that, but the reduced fee for the vaccinations on those days fell below the standard rate. Thousands of people gratefully stood in line to use the community service. Still, there were more than a few who fabricated excuses for not complying with the law. That's why veterinary associations hired and deputized a rabies inspector to follow up and request proof of vaccination.

I cannot speak to the character of any of the inspectors in other counties. But, the man who worked with us for several years was quite, shall I say, colorful. I'm pretty sure our "representative" didn't do much to help the reputation of the veterinary profession.

And the system had some inherent flaws. One of those flaws was the fact that we paid the inspector according to the number of citations he wrote. Yes, we created a conflict of interest for him. For us, it was just a bad investment because the quotes we paid for far outnumbered the resulting vaccines we gave. For one thing, anyone could claim the animal in their yard, barn, or even inside their house had just wandered up and must belong to someone else.

11 LESSONS LEARNED THE HARD WAY

Leave your simple ways, and you will live; walk in the way of insight. Proverbs 9:6

Challenges pour into every day at blinding speed for practicing veterinarians. That creates enormous problems for introverts like me who, by default, need time to ruminate before giving advice or taking action. That's not intended to be an excuse for errant decisions. But, it does mean those two factors subtly work together to escalate the stress level. (By the way, statistically, most veterinarians are introverts.)

It would bore us all to death if this chapter tried to expose an exhaustive list of hard lessons learned over a career. So the following is a list of some major ones which might save someone the trouble of learning through trial and error.

You cannot please everybody.

In our early days of practicing in this profession, I suspect we all believe we'll be the first one ever to impress every client. This one is first because that myth gets smashed in short order.

There were more than a few clients who, according to Vicky, "Cannot be pleased with a pleasing stick." No doubt, someone's face just came to your mind that fits that description, right?

God blessed our family with a first-class pediatrician. Dr. Walker cared for Laura, Matt, and Julie for many years. His professionalism, intelligence, wisdom, and demeanor were so good that he became my personal model of who I wanted to be as a professional. It was difficult for me to imagine anyone ever saying anything negative about Dr. Walker. But one day it happened, and I heard a parent fuming about something he'd said to them. Hopefully, it had no effect on Dr. Walker, but it was a significant moment for me. I realized that if Dr. Walker couldn't please everyone, the pressure was off of me. That "moment" is still helping me to this day.

Communication is hard work.

As Brenda handed me the patient record, she said, "This poor dog's got a huge lump right between his shoulder blades." Quickly, a differential diagnosis of tumor or abscess popped into my mind while I motioned Ms. Do-it-yourself back to the exam room.

The fact that this was, in fact, a large abscess was not unusual, but that was only a small part of the story. A few questions of the history-taking portion of my routine protocol opened a flow from a chain of events leading up to this pus-filled subcutaneous balloon on the back of my patient.

It seems Ms. Do-it-yourself had stopped by the office a week or so ago to pick up a dose of worm medicine for her 70-pound mixed-breed guard dog. As usual, we dispensed the 7 ml of liquid dewormer in a syringe complete with a plastic cap and instructions to give the entire amount by mouth at home.

For reasons still a mystery to me, Ms. DIY decided to go by the local farmer's coop and buy a needle for the syringe. Taking it all home, she'd used the needle to inject the medication under the loose skin between the shoulders of her beloved pet. Those actions proved to be a highly efficient way to create an abscess of rather massive proportions.

Fortunately, Ms. DIY and I were able to remain calm and preserve our long-term client relationship. The treatment was a success, the pet made a full recovery, and we all learned some valuable lessons.

For me, the lesson was to never assume clients will remember how they gave medicine the last time they used it, hear instructions, or read a label.

Transfer clients will transfer again.

There is always a fairly steady stream of "Leap-doc" clients. They'd come in with a perfectly healthy small pet under one arm and a stack of records from the previous practice. Most of the time the complaints, which were quite minor, had mushroomed in their mind to nightly news material. The only way to handle those is to listen with a smile, refuse to say or agree with anything derogatory about a colleague, then give the pet your best effort.

For a while, it seemed this was an excellent way to grow our practice. After all, we now had inside information about what would be displeasing to this client, and all we needed to do was avoid the same mistakes.

About half the time that plan worked, and we did indeed form a long-term relationship. But, at least half the time the leaper would be overcome with the urge to mount a new search for perfection and the burgeoning stack of records would head out the door.

Without a doubt, my friend and colleague, Dr. Barry Stewart, told the most astonishing story of a "Leap-doc" client I've ever heard.

Mr. "Blindly mad" stomped into his clinic one morning thinking he was at PAH. He proceeded to berate Dr. Stewart loudly. The catch is, he thought he was talking to me even though I was a mile up the road working at PAH, which has no resemblance to Hartselle Animal Clinic. I only wish I could have been there to see the man's face when Dr. Stewart helped him get his bearings!

Outdoor signage is an essential business matter.

Until recently there was no business management instruction in the veterinary medicine curriculum. That's not a complaint because the education I received at Auburn was fantastic. However, the lack of training in business management created an unexpected challenge for my colleagues and me.

While there was no business administration training, we did get a significant exposure to professional ethics, which I thoroughly enjoyed. Unknowingly, we were on the cusp of substantial changes in professional ethics. Our professors instructed us that any form of advertising beyond yellow page ads was considered unethical for veterinarians, human physicians, and lawyers. Professionals grew their practices by rendering quality service that stimulated positive word-of-mouth recommendations.

I now realize that I took that philosophy a little too seriously. Hence, the original sign in front of the "new" PAH on Highway 31 in Hartselle was drab and almost camouflaged. The stainless steel letters attached to a dark brown brick wall made it unlikely very many of the thousands of motorists passing by every day could read the name of our business. Even so, we grew at a commendable rate on the strength of word-of-mouth advertising during the next decade.

Finally, in the late eighties, we erected a colorful, large sign that clearly identified our name and function. That sign alone was responsible for a surge in clients as well as a renewed sense of pride within our veterinary staff.

Still, I cringe when I watch attorneys, pharmacies, and human hospitals dominate the commercial segments of the evening TV newscasts. Even though I realize the reason is mostly economical, I'm thankful it's rare to see a commercial highlighting a veterinary hospital.

People like you more than you think they do.

These words would never have made it into print before I retired. Well, make that "pretty much" retired since I recently went back to work part-time. For one thing, my superstitious side would have convinced me that writing it would be some sort of jinx. But more importantly, it's just hard for most of us to see our blessings in the midst of the battle. Plus, we don't appreciate many of those blessings until they are out of reach.

We currently live in Limestone County, which is across the Tennessee River from PAH in Morgan County. Who would have thought that a river bridge could make so much difference? After six-plus years of living in Athens, a few people have begun to realize I'm a veterinarian. It honestly does not offend me to be referred to as Mr. Pearson. However, anyone who addresses me that way is unintentionally saying, "I don't know a thing about your story." And I still tell Connie, half-kiddingly, that I don't "speak Athens."

Now every time we head south across the river bridge into Morgan County, it's like returning to "my people." If the Lord wills, we will move back there. Every time we are in Morgan County, we encounter individuals who do know a lot about "our story."

Just last week while practicing at County Line Veterinary Services in Danville, AL, a former PAH client from many years ago said with an affirming smile, "Dr. Pearson, what are you doing here?" In a nanosecond, our conversation moved forward on the strength of a shared history. Repeating similar encounters has convinced me that, indeed, people saw me in a more favorable light than I ever imagined.

My only reason for including these words is for encouragement to whoever may read them. Trust me, things are never as bad as they seem, and people do like you more than you think they do.

(Connie and I finally moved back to Hartselle in August of 2017. We're home once more.)

Dogs bite, cats scratch, and farm animals kick.

As I looked at my right arm, it was hard to believe what just happened in a matter of seconds. There was no time to dwell on the four-inch laceration and deep puncture wound in my forearm. As I helplessly watched, the frightened Great Dane who'd inflicted the wounds proceeded to ram the front door open as he pulled away from my grip on his collar. We all held our collective breaths as we witnessed the miracle of that huge canine running across four lanes of early morning traffic without a scratch. No sooner had Vicky put "Big Boy" into a run than he had jarred the latch loose and escaped to retrace his steps to the front of the clinic. From that day on, we locked those latches with leash snaps.

You'd think that after practicing for a year with Dr. Bentley, I'd have known about the perils of cat claws. But, early one morning, back on Main Street it became apparent one more lesson was in order. A six-month-old yellow tabby kitten was dropped off for a treatment of skin lesions on his belly. While Vicky held him on his back on the exam table, I placed my face within inches to get a good look. Instantly, that kitten was firmly attached to my face with 16 sharp claws embedded in my skin. We got a good laugh as I wiped streams of blood from my cheeks and thanked the Lord my eyes were not damaged.

When you find clients who you like and respect at a deep level, you naturally want to give your best effort. Mr. Fowler was one of those clients. When meeting this retired schoolteacher whose demeanor communicated his level of education and respectability, you'd never expect him to be a cattle farmer. Mr. Fowler did, in fact, own a few head of well-kept Black Angus on a small farm just outside the city limits. One hot and humid June Saturday right after we closed the office at noon, I responded to his call to examine a cow with a lame rear leg. Of course, being the responsible person he was, the 900-pound patient was already confined in a cattle chute waiting for my arrival.

Wanting to impress Mr. Fowler, I strode to the rear leg and lifted it up to examine the tissue between the cleft hooves knowing that a condition called "foot rot" was the most likely cause of the lameness. The smarter plan would have been to raise the foot by using the rope 20 feet away in the bed of my truck. Things were going well until my probing with the hoof knife touched the intensely sore spot where the infection was near the surface. Suddenly my arms became like pedals on a bicycle as that cow kicked back and forth and my pride refused to let my hand turn loose of that bovine foot.

Although I finished treating Mr. Fowler's cow that day, by the next morning sharp pains deep in my lower back made it almost impossible to get out of bed and go to church.

The next month brought visits to the doctor, an epidural for spinal x-rays, a hospital stay, and injections of steroids. Finally, Mr. Sam Minor, who owned the local furniture store, convinced me to try his vibrating recliner. That's when this episode of a lesson learned the hard way finally came to a close.

12 TOP NINE DO-OVERS I WISH I HAD

Whoever watches the wind will not plant; whoever looks at the clouds will not reap. ... Sow your seed in the morning, and at evening let your hands not be idle, for you do not know which will succeed, whether this or that, or whether both will do equally well. Ecclesiastes 11:6

It would be natural and logical, I guess, to title this chapter "Regrets." But, it's not the title because such a word would imply an incorrect message. God is sovereign, and God is good. All things happen, or don't happen, for a reason. So, while there are some thoughts here about what I think would have been better choices during my years at PAH, I'm equally content that God's been in control through it all.

Mr. Loy Greenhill recently passed away. He was the principal of Crestline Elementary for many years, including when our Laura, Matt, and Julie were students there. He was extraordinary at what he did as an educator and thousands of students benefited from his leadership. After his death, Mr. Greenhill's daughter shared that his actions were guided by the phrase, "And then some…" In other words, he believed in always adding a little more when it would have appeared his job was done. I think that's reliable guidance for any of us who want to make a positive contribution to our sphere of influence.

So here are some challenges we faced, and how I think I would handle them differently if I had the chance.

I'd raise my fees 10% and pay my people more.

One of the hallmarks of PAH is longevity. Key staff stayed for over ten years. Each one of them contributed in tangible and intangible ways that made the experiences so special. It's not that they weren't paid a fair amount at the time. But, it never occurred to me to raise fees specifically to pay them more. If I could do it over, that's what I'd like to do.

I'd be more careful in choosing associates.

From the beginning, my dream was to have a business partner. Connie and I bought a framed painting years ago of three Redheaded Woodpeckers because it reminded me of the ultimate goal of becoming a three-doctor practice. Both eventually happened when Dr. Phil Gault became a partner, and Dr. David Crouch joined us as an associate. That prophetic woodpecker picture still hangs in the study at PAH.

But the road to the dream was not a straight one without challenges and hard lessons. The pursuit of the right fit saw five veterinarians work for various periods of time. Most of them proved to be honest and upright colleagues who made positive contributions and then moved on to practice in other areas. Only one turned out to be a disappointment. Even that somewhat scary experience taught me a lot about people and that I needed to be more diligent in protecting our practice. It also showed me that things are never as bad as they seem at the time.

After going through all of that, I knew how to appreciate Dr. Gault when he finally came along. I remain convinced that every step of the way and his ultimately becoming a full partner in PAH was "a God thing." From the beginning, we connected on a spiritual as well as professional level. And, our families were priorities for both of us.

I'd put more effort into marketing my practice.

My dear late mother-in-law used to say, "He who toots not his own horn, the same shall not be tooted."

"Tooting my own horn" is not in my nature at all. The problem is that I tend heavily in the opposite direction. Of course, no one likes an arrogant attitude, either.

The critical lesson to learn is that marketing and bragging are not the same things. No business can succeed without a marketing plan. Survive maybe, but not thrive. I've already mentioned the lesson learned about the sign in front of our hospital. I don't believe there were ever any business cards printed for PAH, either.

Our ad in the yellow pages was always modest. We never appeared in any of the local football team program ads. My reason was, "We can't be in all of them, so we just won't be in any of them." The real reason was my lack of appreciation for marketing.

These days the Internet makes marketing far easier and far more critical for veterinary practices to thrive. I've heard it said, and I believe it's true, "Without a website your business doesn't exist in today's world." Plus, a weak website is not much better than no website. If I still owned a vet practice, a good website would take first place on my priority list.

I'd communicate more with colleagues.

Although the word itself may not appear hundreds of times in the Bible, numerous stories describe negative consequences of pride. From my current point of view, it's clear to me that I was too proud to stay in touch with other veterinarians who practiced nearby. It was fear of looking stupid or somehow not measuring up that kept me isolated. It seemed like a safe way to live, but in reality, it caused me more stress, and I missed opportunities to learn.

Of course, there were other reasons, too, like raising three kids, commitment to staying involved in our church, and after-hours emergencies many nights a week. Still, if I could go back, I'd make an effort to attend more local meetings and visit other clinics once in a while.

I'd maintain some ownership in the practice longer.

We sold PAH to Dr. Gault and Dr. Crouch in September 2002 just before we left for Cuenca, Ecuador, to serve as missionaries. It's all worked out well, of course, but given a chance to do it over, I'd give more consideration to other options that might have allowed me to maintain at least some ownership.

If we had done so, maybe I'd have felt comfortable moving back to Hartselle instead of Decatur and eventually to Athens. Perhaps we could have kept that three-doctor practice or possibly expanded beyond that. Maybe I wouldn't find myself 15 years later trying to sell a house on the river and move back to Hartselle.

But then I wouldn't have six years' experience working in a corporate veterinary practice. And I doubt I would have found the time or inclination to discover my new passion for writing.

I'd delegate a lot more work.

As I turned the key and opened the metal door that led directly into the kennel, the loud barking of awakening dogs did not affect my thought process. The goal every morning was getting to the office before anyone else arrived. I needed some alone time to prepare myself for the day ahead. I was like a professional weight lifter going through a routine of mental preparation before attempting to set a new personal record for pushing an astonishing burden of cold hard metal above his head.

By the end of a typical day, I'd experience a gratifying tiredness. I'd spay dogs and surgically repair a fractured femur. I'd examine ten pets for their annual visit and check parasite tests on them. Then I'd see a few sick ones, try to answer questions for clients who'd left messages for a return call, help restrain patients for x-rays, and insert iv catheters. Then I'd call a vendor or two to find the best deals on a long list of drugs, vaccines, and related needs.

By the end of the day, most of my physical and mental energy was spent, and I'd be running on reserves by the time I pulled into the driveway at home. Until an emergency hospital opened in Decatur, at least half the time one or two trips back to the hospital for after-hours calls interrupted what free time might have been waiting.

Reading what I just wrote makes me feel pretty stupid. There were people right with me who could have quickly been trained to perform much of what I insisted on doing myself. Honestly, my reasoning for not delegating tasks sooner still eludes me. The good news is that I finally understood the concept and improved at least some in the art of training and delegating tasks.

I'd hire Dr. Stewart knowing he might open a clinic nearby.

I can almost hear the Katydids in the trees on that hot summer afternoon as Dr. Barry Stewart and I sat in lawn chairs in our front yard on Moss Chapel Road. Connie kept the kids busy inside so that the only interruption to our conversation was an occasional carload of teenagers flying by as they raced down "Thrill Hill."

We'd agreed to meet and discuss the possibility of him joining PAH as an associate veterinarian shortly after graduating from veterinary school. My long-term goal was to take on a partner, and he knew joining a practice could be advantageous for him in lots of ways. I was ready to make him an offer, and I believe he wanted to accept it. But there was a proverbial elephant in the room. Before going any further, there was one more obstacle that required a resolution.

The issue, of course, was what would happen if things didn't work out as planned, and we had to part ways later. Out of respect for Dr. Stewart's abilities and connections in Morgan County, I thought it could damage PAH if he stayed awhile, and then opened his practice nearby.

He understood my concerns. The integrity instilled in him by his Dad, Frank Stewart, came through without hesitation. He was candid, saying he could not promise me he'd leave Hartselle to set up practice at some point. A short time later I got a call from Barry letting me know he'd bought some property a mile down the road where he'd soon be opening his practice. I sincerely congratulated him and wished him well. We've been fast friends ever since.

If I could go back to that afternoon, I'd give more consideration to taking the chance of offering him a job as an associate with plans to eventually become a partner. At least he would have been honest and let me know ahead of time if he ever decided to open his practice in Hartselle. A few years later, with a different associate, that didn't happen. Instead, plans developed without my knowledge, and suddenly an associate opened a new practice nearby.

After some serious anxiety and worry, as the months passed by, it became apparent PAH was going to be just fine, after all.

The lesson learned: work hard, be honest, be yourself, and trust God through the hard times. He will provide your needs.

I'd implement more of my ideas…

Expand the facilities

"Hey Dr. Pearson, are you 'gonna bid on the lot next door?" After news spread about the upcoming auction of an acre next to our hospital, I heard that question a lot. The truth is, fear of debt clouded my vision of the future. Soon, when a client came by to describe what grand plans he had after buying the property, he convinced me that the retail business he was going to open there would be like a magnet for new PAH clients. That was enough to keep me away from the auction. Unfortunately, the building still standing next to PAH is more of an eyesore than an attraction.

116

I'd be more involved with practice management.

January 1982 brought a wicked combination of ice and snow that shut down North Alabama for days. Suddenly, I found myself with an overwhelming amount of free time. Those days became a crucial turning point in my professional life. Sitting in a comfortable chair watching slow-burning logs created a perfect atmosphere for reflection and assessment.

Soon I started writing my thoughts about my vision for PAH. I listed goals for 1, 2, 5, and 10 years. Then came ideas of how to get to those goals. Those hours clarified my vision in many intangible ways that made a profound difference in what happened in the years afterward. At least two very tangible changes grew out of what I wrote during that winter storm.

Realizing the value of PAH employees and their unique perspectives, we called a brainstorming meeting for the express purpose of making PAH a better place for clients, pets, and employees. As a result, we soon remodeled and expanded the hospital, painted the walls in more attractive colors, and devised a more flexible work schedule.

After spending money on a veterinary consulting firm, it became clear that practice management boils down to collecting facts and applying common sense to interpret and implement what you already know.

If I could go back, I'd pare down my clinical work and focus more on practice management.

I'd write a training manual and job descriptions.

Only twice in twenty years did Vicky threaten to quit. The first involved a long overdue raise. Then there was the day she said, "OK Doc, either he goes, or I go. Which is it going to be?"

The "he" she referred to was a young Hispanic man who I'd hired because our associate pastor asked me to help him out by giving him a job. He didn't speak a lot of English and certainly had no prior exposure to a veterinary practice. Now I understand more about the cultural differences that doomed the arrangement from the start.

The final crisis came when Vicky asked him to go to the kennel and bathe a dog scheduled to go home in the afternoon. By the time Vicky checked on him to see what was taking so long, he'd washed every dog in the kennel! Understandably, that represented the last straw for Vicky.

I knew training of new employees is indispensable. Writing job descriptions and allowing time for training was on my list of good ideas. Apparently, neither had made it past the right intentions stage. The result was a failure to help a young man when he needed help.

I'd worry less and enjoy more.

My eyes popped open at 3:10 AM and an uneasy, hot feeling spread across my shoulders. This sensation was a far too familiar experience that would practically eliminate any chance for healthy sleep the rest of the night.

The stimulus for worry that night was a dearly loved Boston Terrier. Roscoe needed a molar extraction, and I was confident that procedure was within my capabilities and experience. That was true in most cases. But I'd overlooked the particular challenges of treating brachycephalic breeds like him. The skull, jawbones, and larynx of those animals present unique dangers and obstacles. I learned the hard way the delicate task of removing all of the deep-seated three roots of such a molar.

I'd spent far longer than expected in sawing the tooth into three sections so I could get out each root independently. Trying to pull the tooth intact would likely cause a fractured mandible. Even while working as carefully as possible, one of the roots broke off, leaving a small piece deep on the bone. Not retrieving it might cause a new set of problems, so I spent more time digging into the socket to free the stubborn remaining fragment.

I worried that night if Roscoe was enduring severe pain after the drugs wore off. Was he at home screaming out and keeping his family awake? Would I need to refer him to a dental specialist in Birmingham to correct my inadequacies? Would his family ever forgive me? How many clients would we lose when they heard this story?

Why didn't I refer him in the first place? Frightening questions buzzed in my head like a swarm of pesky mosquitoes on a humid creek bank.

Oh, what a relief it was when Roscoe's dad assured me both he and his family had a normal, peaceful night. And, an hour earlier Roscoe gobbled up the soft food we'd prescribed. Keeping my voice as routine as possible, I reminded them not to miss any of his antibiotics or pain pills. A week later at his follow-up appointment, everything was back to normal.

I must regretfully admit that anxious nights like this often occurred over the years. And no, the days were not worry-free either. Now it's easy to imagine countless hours that I could have filled with enjoyment instead of worrying.

13 THE BEST AND THE WORST ABOUT BEING A VETERINARIAN

The thief comes only to steal and kill and destroy; I have come that they may have life, and have it to the full. John 10:10

As they say, "It's tempting to believe the grass is always greener on the other side." But, I favor the quip, "The grass is greener where it gets watered."

No matter where you go to work tomorrow, you're going to encounter some good and some bad aspects. Life is a lot sweeter when we focus on the good. Over time, the bad stuff morphs into good by teaching us lessons not learned by any other method.

I spent some time trying to decide which to write first. In the end, the best won out in hopes it'll be "green grass" enough to overpower the worst that came to mind.

The Best

Opportunities to build relationships with people

That may seem strange to some. But, for me, it soars to the top of the list. Walk with me through a few conversations during the first ten minutes of a typical day at a vet practice.

"Good morning, Vicky. How's Brent [her young son] feeling today? Sure hope it's just a cold and not the flu. By the way, thanks for cleaning up that mess I left in the surgery last night. It was so late when I finished; I just didn't have the energy to clean it myself."

In an urgent voice, Vicky responds, "Doc, you better call Ms. Johnston before you do anything else. She's worried sick because Roscoe's scratched his ear raw even with the medicine you prescribed. Now that she's a widow, I'm sure it's hard for her to get the solution into his ear canal by herself."

"Good morning, Brenda. I see you scheduled some extra time for the Blankenship appointment. I'm so glad you did because it's not going to be easy to put down Slinky after living with him for 16 years. He's a good cat, but we all know his quality of life is gone now."

Multiply that typical ten minutes by 55-hour weeks for 30 years to get a picture of one aspect of vet practice. Sure glad it's the best part!

Forty-plus years later, I get to hear time after time, "Hey Dr. Pearson. Good to see you. We used to bring our pets to you when I was just a kid."

Streams of chances to help people and their pets

The veterinary practice involves a unique triad of doctor, patient, and client. That means every phone call, every appointment, and every emergency is an opportunity to help a person and an animal.

Of course, every client connects to his or her pets. And, naturally, that connection is more profound for some than for others. One client developed a deep bond more quickly than anyone I ever knew. I first met Julie Johnston on a scorching Sunday afternoon in the pasture in front of her family's home. Her pony was in labor, and she talked to her as though she was her child. I'm convinced that her calming and encouraging voice helped that pony relax enough for me to deliver her foal manually.

There's no telling how many pets she brought into the clinic over the years, and she always expressed the same deep bond with each one, even with hunting dogs that belonged to her dad. Like many other clients, I always knew helping her animals was the same as helping her.

I remember a short period around 1979 to 1980 when clients came in seeking help for a non-animal problem. That's when gasoline prices suddenly spiked, and all manner of rumors broke out about how to increase miles per gallon for vehicles. One popular theory catching on was taping two magnets along opposite sides of the engine's gas line. (Believe it or not, magnets about the size of an index finger are given to cows to swallow like a big pill. The hope is that any metal objects picked up while grazing will connect to the magnet and make it through the GI tract without puncturing the stomach.)

For a few weeks, demand for those magnets was high. Mrs. Henderson reported that she'd verified the better mileage by filling her tank at precisely the same pump and running the numbers. It's doubtful the magnets paid for themselves, and the fad soon disappeared.

Learn and practice unique skills

Have you noticed how many doctors it takes to treat a human patient for anything more dangerous than the sniffles? On the one hand, this makes me feel a little annoyed. On the other hand, I feel bad for them because it seems boring. Unlike today, most of my years of practice were at a time when referring patients to a specialist was pretty rare. Still vets use knowledge in numerous medical fields every day.

For example, a single case often requires expertise in cardiology, dermatology, parasitology, radiology, pharmacy, dentistry, and surgery. Even what clients think of as a routine visit for "shots" includes a thorough exam of the skin, the bones, the eyes, the ears, the teeth, the heart and lungs, and tests for internal and external parasites. During all of that, clients deserve explanations and instructions on how to care for their pet at home.

One busy Saturday morning, a client brought in a new puppy for a check-up and shots. As soon as I curled back the upper lip of that pup, the pale gums told me that vaccinations were not his immediate need. A simple hematocrit confirmed life-threatening anemia. Vaccinations had no chance of protecting this little fellow until he got a blood transfusion. The slide on the microscope stage supplied the diagnosis. As we often say, "He was eaten up with hookworms." The level of renewed energy after a few milliliters of fresh blood always amazes clients. I still get a kick out of that change, too.

At graduation from vet school, the only hands-on orthopedic instruction we had was instruction about various bandage applications. I quickly realized while practicing in Huntsville with Dr. Bentley that injured pets often needed more advanced procedures to heal their bones. He taught me how to stabilize femoral fractures with stainless steel pins placed into the marrow of the bones. Sometimes we formed external casts using flexible aluminum rods. I learned how to remove the head of a femur when the fracture was in that area and a few more methods of fracture repair.

(Because much of our clientele lived in rural areas, and pets roamed free a lot, severe injuries from things like being hit by a car, fights, snakebites, and poisonings (among other things) was more common than one might expect.)

I never dreamed I'd learn to repair fractures using external pins. "Max" Orr put me into that procedure when he encountered a truck and fractured his left tibia in several places. Because an IM (intramedullary) pin could not hold the fragments steadily enough, we ordered an external fixation kit. It worked so well, quite a few patients followed in his footsteps.

Encounter a variety of challenges every day

No two days are alike in a veterinary practice. For that matter, no two hours are alike. On many days I've treated a 2000 pound bull, a 1200 pound horse, a 100 pound Great Dane, and a litter of 8 ounce Teacup Poodles. Boredom is never a problem in a busy practice.

Nothing can top the day a client strolled in with an 8-week-old tiger cub for vaccinations and deworming. Without a doubt that was one of the most beautiful animals I've ever seen. Weighing 25 pounds at the time, it acted as crudely as any kitten that age. Mark and I had a lengthy discussion that afternoon about long-term care for

Tigger. Among other things, he promised to build a suitable pen behind his trailer out at Cedar Cove. Unfortunately, no pen ever materialized, Tigger got used to trailer life, and Mark's wife left him.

We didn't see Mark or Tigger much after he was fully-grown. We did, however, hear reports of the two of them in Mark's pickup truck and one appearance at a local high school football game. (Hartselle's mascot is the tiger.) As far as I know, that's true.

Early on a Wednesday morning, I got a call from Mark. He was so upset and crying so hard it was tough to understand everything he said. But, I got enough to know Tigger's injuries were severe from being hit by a pickup truck on the road near the trailer.

When we arrived at the clinic, Tigger had suffered numerous serious injuries, had lost lots of blood and was in shock. After giving some consideration to trying to make the 200-mile trip to the vet school at Auburn, Mark decided euthanasia would be the kindest thing for Tigger.

I can't help but try to imagine the reaction when the driver of the truck that hit Tigger explained to his boss at work why he was late that morning.

Benefit from an identity as a professional

Please forgive me for using a cliché here. But I need it to make a point about losing something as valuable as an identity. So, here we go. "You don't know what you've got until you don't have it anymore."

For 30 years, people in Hartselle referred to me as Dr. Pearson. They knew I was a local veterinarian. They knew my family. They knew the location of my clinic. Many of them had a common bond with me through their animals. They had an opinion (mostly good, I hope) about my character and integrity. They knew they could call on me with any issue with an animal. Who wouldn't love that? The day was coming when I'd realize I hadn't appreciated it nearly enough.

Thinking I'd practice right there in Hartselle for at least 10 to 20 more years, it was easy to take something like that for granted. Then in January 2002, Connie and I committed our lives to following a call from the Lord to pursue serving as missionaries overseas. It was a grueling year of praying, seeking, and making hard decisions day after day. In September 2002, we signed the paperwork and sold PAH to Dr. Gault and Dr. Crouch. Filled with excitement about this "great adventure" God had led us to, we spent the next two-plus months preparing for the transition to what was ultimately Cuenca, Ecuador.

Once there, we gradually realized we no longer enjoyed an identity. We should have seen that coming, but we didn't. It was understandable that the people of Ecuador couldn't know anything about us, but even fellow missionaries had no history with us, either. On the rare occasion someone might refer to me as Dr. Pearson, it seemed hollow and carried no indication of a common bond.

Now that we've moved back to Hartselle and I'm working one day a week at County Line Veterinary Services in Danville, it feels like I've recovered most of my identity.

The Worst

Effects on the family

Practicing vets in small towns have no time to call their own. That's better now because of the availability of emergency clinics to take care of pets after hours, on weekends, and holidays. For most of my years at PAH, emergency clinics were not a reality yet.

I'm not sure why, but we kept the telephone receiver on Connie's side of the bed. She became pretty good at giving me a heads up after speaking with a client in the middle of the night. Sometimes she'd punch me and say, "Sounds like eclampsia." In nursing dogs that's a condition where the calcium levels in the blood fall too low and cause seizures. It requires an immediate infusion of calcium into the vein, so she'd know I was about to make a trip to the office.

I doubt there is a single hour out of the 24 on the clock that I never went back for some emergency.

As the kids grew up and our time together got interrupted so much, I'd try to convince them to go with me. They liked going on farm calls once in a while. On one occasion when the call was to a cow in labor, I enticed them with a promise to go to McDonald's afterward for an ice cream cone. By the time I finished the job, my clothes and my body reeked. In fact, they insisted we go straight home and forget the ice cream.

On a pleasant Sunday afternoon, Mr. Elmer Thompson needed me to come out and see about his milk cow with mastitis. He never realized I was the grown-up kid he'd buzzed with .22 bullets for frog gigging in his pond several years before. He and Mrs. Thompson loaded the kids up with fresh eggs and a couple of baby chicks each before we could leave.

We always made eating supper together a priority in our family. Connie has a knack for keeping the conversation lively, and we had many precious hours during and after evening meals. Most nights included them listening to me carry on a telephone conversation with a client. They say they remember me asking questions like, "How much blood is there?" Or, "How long are the worms you're seeing?" Or, "What color is the poop when it comes out?"

It's not helpful to think about how many hours of family time I missed over the years. And, the kids turned out to be fantastic adults with kids of their own. Maybe my intermittent absence turned out all right after all.

By the way, none of the three kids ever considered pursuing a veterinary career. I guess they wanted to be home more and sleep through the night uninterrupted.

Stress

Most people will be surprised to learn that members of the veterinary profession commit suicide at a higher rate than the general public. Rates of burnout, anxiety, and depression also rank considerably high among veterinary practitioners.

The mingling of severe levels of stress within such a gratifying profession forms an intriguing paradox. Once a practitioner learns to embrace the tension and focus on the positive aspects, the upside far outweighs the downside.

The next time you visit your vet, please remember some of the things they may be dealing with and be as kind to them as you are to your pets.

14 HOW VETERINARY MEDICINE HAS CHANGED DURING THE PAST 46 YEARS

Then God said, "Let us make mankind in our image, in our likeness, so that they may rule over the fish in the sea and the birds in the sky, over the livestock and all the wild animals, and over all the creatures that move along the ground." Genesis 1: 26-27

The Lord God took the man and put him in the garden of Eden to work it and take care of it. Genesis 2:15

What other profession gets to flesh out these two biblical mandates from God? Like the name of the first Book of the Bible implies, these words are only the beginning point, the foundation of why veterinarians exist and function. I believe the more we know, understand and apply the entire Bible, the better equipped we'll be to fulfill and enjoy our work of caring for animals.

Core beliefs about animals and escalating expectations.

During my lifetime, the status of animals in our culture has steadily skyrocketed. Since I graduated from vet school in 1972, the social position of pets like dogs and cats has changed exponentially. Back then, almost no one would admit to sleeping with a pet. Now, people who don't share their bed with a pet are considered suspect.

The human-animal bond is a unique and fascinating relationship. Currently, pets are considered family members by a vast majority of animal caretakers.

Naturally, the demand for advanced medical care grows along the same upward curve. Scientific expansion trickles down directly to local veterinarians. That demands the purchase of new equipment and learning how to use it.

Sometimes all this puts new pressure on private practices because new technology comes with loads of associated increased costs. The reality is, many clients fail to understand and expect to benefit without paying equivalent increases in veterinary fees. I'm optimistic it will level out eventually, but the unbalanced paths to equilibrium create some turbulence along the way.

Cost of education, numbers of veterinarians, and barriers to small businesses

Throughout my years of involvement with veterinary medicine, there's been an ongoing debate about whether there is a glut or a shortage of veterinary practitioners. The correct answer depends on how many practices there are within your particular market area.

But there is no debate about whether the cost of a veterinary education is far too high. Average students have for the past 10-15 years graduated with crippling amounts of debt. Studies show that it's economically better to graduate with a BS degree and far less debt than to graduate with a DVM degree and the typical level of debt. Lots of academic, professional, and government entities are working to solve the problem, but at this point, a lasting solution is not in place.

Perception of value and declining loyalty

Every day for 17 years I arrived at work wearing a necktie. That, and a white lab coat were expected by veterinary clients back then. It was a simple yet profound way to give clients a perception of value because veterinary medicine was a doctor-centric profession.

Neckties and white lab coats would send a more negative message now. At least half the profession now is female, and almost all the men have traded ties for polo shirts or scrubs. Clothing matters far less now because veterinary medicine has become a patient-centric profession.

Projecting a perception of value is far more complicated now, too. Clients look for a multitude of services and products for their pets. More and more of those are available from places outside a veterinary practice. Clients want to be more educated about pet health care, and veterinarians have to be aggressive to be their source of information. Will they get the information from a questionable Internet source, or will veterinarians provide it for them through a website and social media?

Client loyalty still exists, and it's as valuable to clients, pets, and doctors as it ever was, but the forces pulling against it seem to multiply on and on. Proximity is not much of an advantage now because most clients live the same distance from 3 or 4 clinics. The key to establishing loyalty is getting the entire staff to invest a lot of intentional effort to stay connected to clients. The good news is, social media and websites are powerful tools to help accomplish the task.

Regardless, no matter how much change takes place, no matter how far science advances, veterinary medicine will always remain a beautiful way to make a living!

15 SHOULD YOU CHOOSE A VETERINARY CAREER?

For You created my inmost being; You knit me
together in my mother's womb. I praise You
because I am fearfully and wonderfully made; Your
works are wonderful, I know that full well.
Psalm 139: 13-14

How it happened in my case.

Back when I was in high school, families often sat on
the front porch on warm summer nights and just talked to
each other. Sometimes life-changing ideas bubbled up in
that relaxed environment. That's what happened one night
in the summer of 1965, one year before I'd be graduating
and heading down to Auburn University.

My plan had been focused on entering the School of
Forestry, mainly because I knew how much I loved being
in mountains and rivers and anywhere outside the city. As
we talked that night, my Dad reminded me again that
people in forestry spend an awful lot of time behind a desk
instead of tromping through the woods. Okay then, what

should I do instead?

For whatever reason, my younger brother blurted out, "Why don't you go into veterinary medicine?" Immediately I liked the idea. Yes, I did love taking care of pet dogs and cats. And I felt comfortable studying science courses in biology. I realized how much I admired medical people, and the thought of helping people and animals at the same time was very appealing to me. Although I had no way of knowing it, I would also spend lots of time outdoors on cattle farms in the years ahead.

Neither my brother nor I have ever been accused of being "angels," but the evidence is overwhelming that there was Divine intervention that guided me to enter veterinary medicine. And, after all, prayers had been offered to ask for His guidance.

So, is veterinary medicine right for you?

Please don't hold your breath, thinking the next few lines will answer that question for you. Instead, as honestly as you can, answer the following questions as a way to at least help you narrow your options. Try to be open to a variety of careers. Pray for guidance and be patient while you wait for that special moment when you can sense you've discovered what fits you.

1) *What is my brain best suited to study and learn?* Natural science? Physical science? Language and literature? Mathematics? Music? Mechanics? Creative activities? Maybe something else?

As I neared retirement, I wanted to start a new career as a financial planner. Taking online courses to reach that goal made it plain that my brain is not comfortable with the math associated with economic formulas. My comfort zone is in studying natural sciences.

2) *Do I enjoy facing challenges or do I prefer doing familiar things well?*

No one can get through life without facing challenges, of course. But, do you prefer stretching your limits to accomplish new things outside your current abilities? Veterinarians find themselves in that kind of circumstance a lot.

3) *Am I more comfortable as a leader or as a follower?*

Leadership is a fundamental part of life as a veterinarian. Clients come to you expecting answers to their questions. Employees look to you for training, for job security, for job satisfaction, and much more. Each veterinarian plays a role in creating the public perception of our profession.

4) *Do I enjoy interacting with people for long periods of time?*

Love for animals is not sufficient reason to pursue a veterinary career. Veterinarians spend far more time interacting with people than with animals.

That sounds like only extroverts can enjoy practicing veterinary medicine. But statistically, most vets are introverts. As a solid introvert, I do very much enjoy interacting with people of all sorts.

5) *What do I want my family life to look like after graduation?*

Practicing veterinary medicine is very demanding and requires a lot of time and attention. Are you willing to continually battle the demands and find creative ways to spend time with your family while you dedicate big chunks of your time to your career?

6) *Can I see events in my past that could connect with this career?*

Everything in life happens for a reason. Take time to review your past experiences and try to get a general sense of the direction you're already going.

7) *Is it well with my soul?*

Life is not perfect. Time will tell whether decisions we make are good, bad, or somewhere in between.

I spent a lot of time being scared to death and anxious about my abilities to do my job well. Still, most of the time there was a quiet assurance down deep inside of me that kept me on track. That confidence came from knowing God had shaped me, led me, and opened opportunities along the way for me to be who and where I was at the time.

16 DEFINING MOMENTS

The steps of a man are established by the LORD,
when He delights in his way; though he fall, he shall
not be cast headlong, for the LORD upholds his
hand. Psalm 37:23-24

Barely in the black.

To this day Connie often reminds me of what I
convinced her to do one morning about six months after
we opened PAH for business.

We had a mortgage on our home. We were making
payments on the 1962 Chevrolet pickup truck I used for
farm calls. Our veterinary vendors were expecting two
payments every month: one for equipment set up on
monthly payments and another for our monthly orders of
drugs and supplies. Mr. Bill Gardner paid us a visit the first
day of each month to collect rent on the office space we
were working from. Estimated income tax bills arrived for
payment quarterly, and Connie was deep into the "nesting
phase" of her first pregnancy, so we'd bought some
necessary items for the nursery.

I walked in that morning and cautiously checked the

balance in our checkbook. It was nearing the middle of the month and what reached my eyes caused cold sweaty palms and a slight shortness of breath. Our little family business had twenty-five dollars to our name. That was it; there was no secret savings account waiting to bail us out.

Mercifully, thoughts of paying for children's education or weddings or medical bills stayed far from my consciousness. All I knew was that somehow, we had to earn enough in the days ahead to pay every obligation on time. I never considered then, or at any other time, trying to see how long creditors might wait for their payments.

As president of the bank that his family owned, Mr. Horace Broom was a prominent citizen of the Hartselle community, and he managed a cattle farm. Realizing that I'd recently made a trip to his farm and excised a small tumor from the eyelid of one of his cows, the first step to freedom flooded my mind. After finishing the job, he'd asked me to send him a bill. Of course, you can't deny credit to a banker even though everyone else had to pay on the spot for services rendered. Surely, he must know what our bank account looks like, I naively thought. Surely, he'll be glad to pay us the outstanding invoice this morning.

So I sent the most persuasive person I've ever known to walk over to the bank and hand deliver the invoice to Mr. Broom. Amazingly, Connie agreed to do it with no small amount of encouragement from me. I don't know what she said, but he wrote her a check. She then carried the tiny trickle of funds across the room to a bank teller and deposited the money into our account. By God's grace, we never saw our resources reach such a low level again.

I realize now that we could have found it impossible to pay all our obligations that month and many other months if animal owners had not shown up for our services in time. But, we did always manage to have the funds needed to make all our payments on time. Years later, pharmaceutical representatives told me we were unique in that way.

Are we gonna be rich?

I'm sure my feet never touched the steps or the threshold as I dashed into the back door with a newsflash to share with Connie. I don't know how long we'd been open for business at the time, but I do know the day marked a milestone we still fondly remember.

Connie has no problem reading my face and body language. On this day, they must have communicated a mixture of gratification, excitement, and pure happiness. "What is it?" she asked, reacting to the mood in the room. My optimistic response came quickly, and I almost shouted, "We deposited $100 for today's work!"

I know it sounds silly now until you understand a few facts:
1. My take-home pay while working for Dr. Bentley the previous year came to just over $80 a week.
2. Without any knowledge about what the average veterinarian earned, I was hoping we could gross around $18,000 our first year. Getting there by working six days a week would require about $54 a day. (Could we somehow double that goal?)
3. Today's value of $100 after inflation is $568.08.
4. My fees were too low because I mistakenly thought higher charges would cause a loss of business.

If I'd understood the true potential, how busy we'd be in the near future, or how much God was about to bless us, my heart could not have taken it.

Phone calls at family mealtimes.

By the time Laura, Matt, and Julie were old enough to engage in conversations and react independently to experiences around them, we lived just below "Thrill Hill" on Moss Chapel Road. Sitting around the table at mealtimes, especially suppertime, became a firmly-guarded custom for our family. We all cherish those times of unconstrained dialogue.

The table sat just inside wide windows looking out on the backyard and the small valley between the Conway family and us. My chair was nearest the wall where the mustard yellow telephone hung with its extra-long, coiled cord dangling below. More times than not, clients called during a meal. The seating arrangement made it easy for me to answer a call without getting up from the table. As I've mentioned previously, these calls are still remembered by my children for the rather "colorful" questions that were asked and answered.

A call from a local cattle farmer provided a particularly interesting "half-conversation" for them to take in. After giving birth, one of his cows developed a prolapsed uterus which means her entire uterus fell out of her birth canal. My family heard me say, "Is it out far enough to reach the ground? Is she still standing? How much hay and manure are on it? Do you see any torn places? Rinse it off with some warm water and cover it with sugar until I can get there. Keep her and the calf as still as possible so they won't step on it."

For at least a week following one of those conversations, Matt would break any silence with whichever phrase caught his attention the most. To this day you may hear him say, "How far is that thang hanging out?"

The cat that had wings.

Hartselle, Alabama is known for its nationally recognized school system and excellence in athletic accomplishments. Big-time criminal stories and similar unfavorable events occur at rates far below many communities. Of course, we're all grateful and downright proud of such a legacy. However, it must be hard for the local newspaper editor to write stories that maintain respectable circulation numbers. I guess all that played a part in some articles that appeared in the local paper back in the early seventies about a cat that had somehow grown a pair of wings. Naturally, I read the accounts with a great deal of interest, not knowing how sincere the reports were meant to be.

Apparently, a substantial amount of discussion developed at local restaurants, on street corners, and maybe even a few Sunday School classes. As far as I could tell the camps of believers and skeptics were close to equal in numbers. I certainly had my own opinion on the matter but chose to keep my thoughts within our staff.

Before long, I had to break my silence and give an opinion when the editor who'd written the articles came by for professional judgment. I quickly realized he was firmly in the camp of believers.

My initial response of, "There must be a logical explanation because cats simply do not grow wings," was not met with any level of approval. So I took a gentler approach and listened to the proposal that this cat had to be a result of an unprecedented genetic mutation with the prospect of drawing attention from the scientific world. Finally, we agreed that I should accompany the editor just past I-65 to the home of the "flying feline" of Hartselle.

As soon as we arrived, it was clear that I was about to face the task of dishing out disappointing news to a proud and confident owner of a pet cat in extreme need of grooming. It was easy for me to see the source of the "wings" as massive clumps of matted hair, but I had to admit it was pretty amazing how the result appeared to be wings attached to the back, almost symmetrically positioned right where you'd expect to find wings on the body of a bird. My suggestion of clipping away the mats met with firm reluctance. The owner scrunched his shoulders, frowned, and tilted his head as he said, "I don't know doc. I think I'll wait a while and see what happens." I never heard the result, but I do know that marked the end of articles on the "cat with wings" in the newspaper.

Almost killed twice. Yes, I'm serious.

My appreciation for the beauty, strength, and uniqueness of horses matches that of anyone. I'd ridden a few during my childhood and teenage years, too. But I'd never understood the danger lurking within close encounters with those magnificent animals.

During the first years of veterinary practice, I was happy to respond to the needs of any animal whenever the opportunity arose. As a result, in addition to pet dogs and cats, I had the chance to treat pigs, goats, sheep, snakes, rabbits, birds (including an Emu), tigers, cattle, and, of course, horses.

My first frightening experience came with a call to visit a nearby farm to draw blood from a horse. The Coggins Test only requires a few milliliters of blood, the jugular vein of a horse bulges into view with slight pressure on the neck, and patients rarely react to the sharp needle prick.

Just as was so often the case with horse calls, the owner was busy with other business and couldn't be there when I came out. But, his father-in-law would be there to help me. My patient, a middle-aged mare, was waiting in a small stall. The father-in-law calmly assured me this horse was as gentle as they come, and I should have no problem getting the sample while he waited just beyond the closed wooden door.

The mare was calm and had that familiar barely awake expression contented equines display. Her feet were so still that there was no dust floating around in the air like you'd expect to see from any nervous moving around. But the instant I inserted that needle into the vein, she became a bucking bronco fit for any rodeo. As she swung her body around and around with rear hooves kicking violently in every direction, the stall filled with enough dust to make it hard to see, let alone breathe.

I'll never know how I escaped that stall with no physical injuries, and after the adrenaline in my veins calmed down, the realization of how close I'd just come to severe injury or death settled in. After a few minutes, we walked her outside the stall, applied a nose twitch and quickly drew the blood sample.

The other incident involved a horse as well. It was on a Saturday right after we'd closed the office when a client called requesting an exam of a lame horse at her farm. This farm was upscale, with spacious, modern, neatly painted and kept barns. The owner's knowledge and professionalism made me feel at ease as we approached the paddock holding my patient.

Unfortunately, I unknowingly walked between a mare and her foal. That action naturally sparked a deep-seated reaction of maternal protection from the mama. The next thing I remember is her massive body lunging full-speed in attack mode directly toward me. If she'd been a dragon, long lashes of fire would have been leaping from her nostrils. Once again, I somehow ducked behind a door just in time to avoid serious injury or death. Driving home in my truck that day, I decided that wisdom demanded I end my career as an equine veterinarian.

As you must know by now, I believe in divine intervention. Shortly after that event and subsequent decision, Dr. Jerome Turner opened a practice in nearby Decatur, Alabama. Oh, I almost forgot to mention that he was allergic to dogs and cats and intended to restrict his practice to treating horses and cattle. From then on, all my equine calls were happily referred to him.

17 CHANGE IS NEVER EASY

Choose this day whom you will serve …. But as for
me and my house, we will serve the Lord.
Joshua 24:15

"You can have anything you want, but you can't have everything you want." We all learn sooner or later that there are limits to things and experiences we can obtain in life. In fact, our lives present us with a continuous series of choices from tiny, imperceptible ones to highly impactful ones.

This final chapter is an attempt to describe the decision that led to the end of my experience at PAH.

The seeds of that decision were planted in July 1990 when Connie and I traveled to Niteroi, Brazil with a group from a church in Florence, Alabama. It was the first of several short-term mission trips we made during the following years to various foreign countries. Each one of those journeys proved to be a life-changing event causing us to experience a form of restlessness and an ill-defined spiritual tug toward deeper missionary involvement.

The days of 1998 and 1999 painted a picture of happiness and prosperity. We loved the joys of being involved in beautiful weddings for Laura, Matt, and Julie. Our dream home, nestled on a hillside in the middle of 10 peaceful acres, surrounded by good neighbors in Cedar Cove became "home base" for our expanding and scattering family. Connie's musical skills and her empathetic personality allowed her daily opportunities to influence hundreds of students. Pearson Animal Hospital reached new levels of effectiveness and became an integral part of Hartselle. We enjoyed distinct and gratifying identities individually, as a family, and as a business. The focus of most conversations and concerns centered around "Y2K" because of the perceived threat of a massive computer crash. Beyond that, life was good.

The ramifications of the attacks on the World Trade Center in New York City on September 11, 2001, are too numerous to count, of course. The horrors of that act are undeniable, but we've all heard stories of encouraging results, as well. Like many, my heart longed to do something to strengthen and support our democracy and help stop the threat of terrorism. I believed then, as I do now, that this battle required spiritual combat fought by an army of followers of Jesus Christ.

In January 2002, Connie and I happily accepted a dinner invitation from our friends John and Glen Ingouf who'd recently retired after 38 years of missionary service in Indonesia. A veterinarian and his wife, home from their missionary work in Indonesia, joined us that night. During conversations at the table, we learned how the International Mission Board (IMB) needed a veterinarian to take a position on a farm in Indonesia. At that moment a unique opportunity to join the spiritual battle on the front lines seemed to materialize from nowhere. The situation had the marks of a calling we could not ignore.

Appointment as missionaries for the IMB involves a lengthy and thorough process. After days of solitary and shared time on our knees, we knew it was time for us to contact the agency and take the first steps to determine God's will for our future. Our mantra became, "As long as God opens doors, we'll step forward through each one." Although the "door" to Indonesia closed, another one opened for us to serve in Ecuador.

Before all this, I planned to practice ten more years at PAH, then begin the process of selling PAH and semi-retire. But God had other plans, and His hand was involved long before I even remotely realized it. The most important evidence of that was the presence of my partner, Dr. Gault, and our associate, Dr. Crouch, who were both agreeable to buy the practice so we could pursue our calling to Ecuador. Many veterinarians struggle for years to find suitable buyers for a small animal veterinary practice. That hurdle was divinely overcome months before we encountered it.

Even though most everyone assumed that this was "retirement" for me, it was not. Serving as a missionary is NOT a form of retirement. Instead, it's a whole new career and quite a full-time job.

The obstacles overcome, the agonies, and the victories of the remainder of 2002 deserve another book. Suffice it to say that on December 27, 2002, we boarded a plane bound for Ecuador as newly-appointed IMB missionaries.

My limited ability does not allow me to find sufficient words to describe the mixture of anguish and anticipation triggered by selling PAH and our home, moving away from our family, and losing our identity. But we took the challenge on faith and jumped off the cliff, knowing our Lord would be there to provide everything we needed.

Even now, I know in my heart that step of faith was the right decision. I wouldn't trade the spiritual growth we experienced in Ecuador for anything. And by the way, I'm grateful that Pearson Animal Hospital is still serving people and their pets in Hartselle, Alabama since the beginning days back in April 1973 until today.

ABOUT THE AUTHOR

As the editor and the author's daughter, I couldn't let this chance pass to tell the world about my Dad. Having lived through it (I'm the new baby that caused dancing in the reception area of that first office on Main Street), I can tell you that every word in this book is true.

My Dad is one of the greatest men I have ever known. His integrity is impeccable, his love for Christ is unquenchable, and his sense of humor is legendary. He is devoted to his wife, children, and grandchildren. Each one of the Pearson Cousins is absolutely convinced that he or she is his favorite. And they're all correct.

I love you, Dad. I'm so thankful that you have written this book. I think it's wonderful.

92610424R00088

Made in the USA
Columbia, SC
30 March 2018